BRITAIN'S HAUNTED LAND

Britain's Haunted Land. A watercolour by Edith Massingham, 1899.

JOHN WEST

BRITAIN'S HAUNTED LAND

INTRODUCTION BY
JASON FIGGIS

DB
PUBLISHING

Dedicated to the memory of
M.R. James and Sir Simon Marsden

Cover design: Jason Figgis

Image: Willgard Krause/Pixabay

Tree Spirit: Aeva Andersson

First published 2023 by DB Publishing, an imprint of JMD Media Ltd,
Nottingham, United Kingdom.

ISBN 9781780916439

Printed in the UK

CONTENTS

Now it is the time of night.

That the graves, all gaping wide,

Every one lets forth his sprite.

In the church-way paths to glide.

William Shakespeare, *A Midsummer Night's Dream*

ABOUT THE AUTHOR

John West was born in London. He is a film producer, actor and the author of books and articles on history, crime, ghosts, and folklore. His first book on British ghosts - *Britain's Haunted Heritage* - was published in November 2019. Two new titles, *Britain's Ghostly Heritage* and *The Battle of Gainsborough 1643* followed in 2022.

As a journalist, John currently writes for *Psychic News* and *Suffolk and Norfolk Life*. His features include celebrity interviews and investigations into famous hauntings from the UK and beyond.

In 2018 John teamed up with the director Jason Figgis. He became a producer/publicist on the film, *Simon Marsden: A Life in Pictures*,

John West (Jason Figgis).

before going on to produce and act in Figgis' M.R. James-inspired chiller *The Ghost of Winifred Meeks*. They went on to form Figgis-West, a production company with John co-producing Figgis' *The Grey Man*, *Clare Island*, *The Wedding Ring*, *In Our Day*, *Mythmaker: George A. Romero*, *The Black Widow*, and *Dunkirk 80*.

From 2021 to 2023 the team made four documentaries, *Maverick*, *Shirley Baker: Life Through a Lens*, *The Life and Work of Colin Wilson*, and *Love?* John wrote the narration for Shirley Baker and contributed material to Colin Wilson. Many more projects are planned between the two, including feature films and documentaries on Dracula and Jack the Ripper.

INTRODUCTION BY JASON FIGGIS

When I was asked to contribute a introduction to this latest collection of ghostly manifestations and strange happenings from writer John West, I was intrigued by the title, which conjured up sweeping green meadows shrouded in mist, gnarled branches of moss-laden skeletal trees in quiet woodlands and deserted laneways, and tall hedgerows on either side, gently swaying with whispers of wind, bringing the dense foliage to shivering, breathing life.

There is something particular about the British Isles – and I include Ireland geographically in this respect – that summons thoughts of centuries of rich and violent history that brought kings to their knees in

Jason Figgis (Bernadette Manton).

bloody battle and high priests to their altars in secret worship of forbidden gods. Every field and hilltop, every town and village, has traces – and so much more – of centuries past, and with these indelible memories of what has gone before are passed down myriad tales of ghosts and hauntings and otherworldly experiences.

There is rarely an abbey or great house or castle or cemetery that has no association with rich and varied folklore; of headless horsemen, ghostly maidens, terrifying echoes of gory battles, or spectral monks, tracing their way along prayer paths, as they did in life, that now, in many cases, no longer exist – as evidenced by their shadowy figures disappearing through the walls of perhaps a modern bungalow – now built on the grounds of formerly hallowed places.

Merely standing on the hilltop of any of Britain's high places, which afford, in more cases than not, a breathtaking vista of all that lies before the viewer, it is impossible not to entertain the wealth of history this land has been witness to, and for those willing to entertain the more esoteric tales of Pagan worship and the rich tapestry of the paranormal, then these wondrous views are dotted far and wide with such tales.

Tales which will soon convince us that Britain is indeed a haunted land.

Jason Figgis
Film director – Dublin, Ireland, 2023

OUR HAUNTED LAND

Great Britain is a land full of ghosts. I first discovered this after reading my mother's collection of books on the supernatural as a child. These volumes fed my interest, and it was not long before my father was buying me books such as *Haunted London* by Peter Underwood and Usborne's three-volume set, *The World of the Unknown*. A steady diet of the BBC's M.R. James' *Ghost Stories for Christmas* and Colin Wilson's *Leap in the Dark* TV series cemented that interest, and now, some 45 years later, I am still fascinated by ghosts.

But what are ghosts? Recordings, time slips, or the souls of the dead? Maybe they are none of these, or maybe they are even all three?

During my travels across Britain, I have spoken to countless people who have seen phantom monks, ghostly ladies, and sometimes even Black Shuck, the legendary demon hound of East Anglia. I have also witnessed things that cannot easily be explained away by sceptics as tricks of the light or figments of my imagination. What of the dog that haunted my Lincolnshire home, the poltergeist activity shortly after my mother died, the sudden feeling of terror in Borley churchyard, or the ghost that pulled off my duvet in my flat in Suffolk? These things happened, and the memory of them will stay with me to my dying day.

W. Howells, in his book *Cambrian Superstitions*, published in 1831, had his own interesting and somewhat amusing theories about ghosts: 'In most of the relations of ghosts, they are supposed to be mere aerial beings without substance who can pass through walls and other solid bodies at pleasure. We also read of ghosts striking violent blows, and that if not made way for, they overturn all impedimenta like a furious whirlwind; the usual time for their appearance is midnight, seldom before it is dark, and no ghosts appear on Christmas Eve.

'If, during the time of an apparition, there is a lighted candle in the room, it will burn extremely blue; the coming of the spirit is announced sometime before its appearance by a variety of loud and dreadful noises and is rarely visible to more than one person, although there are several in company.

'A ghost has not the power to speak until it has been first spoken to, so that notwithstanding the urgency of the business on which it may come, everything must stand still till the person visited can find sufficient courage to speak to it.

'The mode of addressing a ghost is by commanding it in the name of the three persons of the Trinity to tell you who it is and what is its business, this may be necessary to repeat three times, after which it will, in a low and hollow voice, declare its satisfaction at being spoken to and desire the party addressing it not to be afraid, for it will do no harm. This being promised, it commonly enters into its narrative, which, being completed and its requests or commands given with the injunction that they will be immediately executed vanishes away, frequently in a flash of light. During the narration of its business, a ghost must by no means be interrupted by questions of any kind, so doing is extremely dangerous; if any doubts arise, they must be stated after the spirit has done its tale. Questions respecting its state are offensive and not often answered.

'If, after the first appearance, the persons employed neglect or are prevented from performing the message or business committed to them, the ghost appears continually to them, at first with a discontented, next an angry, and at length with a furious countenance, threatening to tear them in pieces if the matter is not forthwith executed. Sometimes ghosts appear and disturb a house without deigning to give any reason for so doing, with these, the shortest and only way is to exercise and eject them. For this purpose, there must be two or three clergymen, and the ceremony must be performed in Latin, a language that strikes the most audacious ghost with terror. A ghost may be laid for any term less than 100 years, but of all places, the most common and what a ghost least likes is the Red Sea. It being related in many instances, that ghosts have most earnestly besought the exorcists not to confine them to this space.'

Will we ever learn the answer to what really lies behind the phenomenon of ghosts? I doubt it. I very much expect that we will have to wait until it is our own time to cross the veil before we finally discover the truth. I hope that we will not be disappointed!

John West
2023

Chapter One

THE HAUNTED BYPASS

The town of Stocksbridge lies in South Yorkshire, some seven miles from Sheffield. In the 1980s, a decision was made to build a bypass around the town. When completed, this road would link the A628 with the M1.

Work commenced, and the stretch above Stocksbridge became the scene of strange activity after construction work cut through Pea Royd Lane. The moorland lane became impassable, and a bridge was built to ensure that it could still be used by the public.

It was September 1987, and the bridge was still unfinished, with only the middle section completed. Long ladders provided the only access at this stage.

On September 7, two security men, David Goldthorpe and Steven Brookes, were patrolling the area. They worked for Constant Security Services and had been keeping an eye on the site for two months. It was near midnight, and the pair were driving past an electricity pylon when they saw beneath the structure a group of four or five children dressed in what they described as 'old-fashioned clothes' dancing in a circle. The men stopped and searched the area, but could find no trace of the children. Although the area was muddy, the spot where the children had been dancing was strangely devoid of footprints.

The men continued with their inspection of the building site and made their way back to the bridge. They could see a white figure in a hood standing on the parapet. They drove up a ramp and stopped the car on Pea Royd Lane. The figure was still visible, and David Goldthorpe turned the car headlights on full beam. The light shone right through the figure, and it vanished.

The men were so shocked by their experience that they ended the shift and made their way to nearby Mexborough, where Constant Security was based. They told their boss, Peter Owens, what had happened. He later recalled how shocked they were. One of the men was even in tears as he spoke of what they had seen.

Michael Lee, the managing director and a former policeman, decided to inform the local police in Deepcar. PC Dick Ellis was sceptical of their story but became impressed as they told him of their experience. Both men refused to return to the site until something

A monk-like figure has been seen haunting the Stocksbridge Bypass.

was done. PC Ellis explained that it was not really a police matter and suggested that they seek help from the church. The men then went to the local church and refused to leave until the building site had been exorcised. PC Ellis finally managed to calm them down, and they left. Both men were so shocked by what they had seen that they resigned from their jobs – one after three days and the other a few months later.

PC Ellis decided to look into the matter and did some research at the local library. He also spoke to historians and older members of the community. He found that there was a legend dating back several hundred years about a Cistercian monk who had left a local monastery. He ended up living at Underbank Hall, which lies at the end of the bypass. He vanished after visiting Stocksbridge Market during bad weather and was never seen again. Another story claimed that he was buried in unconsecrated ground in the area of the bypass. The building work was supposed to have disturbed his last resting place.

A further report dated from 150 years earlier and concerned several children who were travelling in a cart down Hunshelf Bank. It had turned over in the area of the later bypass, and all had been killed. However, the policeman was unable to find any documents confirming this in the local historical records.

Two paranormal investigators, Ralph Knutt and David Clarke, also researched the case and discovered that workmen living in the area of the building site had heard children's voices in the night. A recluse living on the hillside had also seen children dancing around a caravan and the electricity pylon.

On September 12, PC Ellis decided to visit the scene of the alleged haunting. The time was midnight. He took Special Constable John Beet with him. He had only told his colleague two hours earlier of his intention to go there. He also refrained from telling his other colleagues at the station, as they may have gone there themselves to play a trick on the pair.

The two officers took a Panda car to the bypass and parked it between the bridge and the pylon. On the bridge was a white pallet box. The sky was clear, and the moon was out. The glare from the steelworks below them cast an eerie orange light on the area as Ellis and Beet turned off all the lights and the radio and waited to see what would happen. The pair noticed a shadow, so they switched on the car headlights. The shadow had gone. They then drove up to the bridge and got out. Nothing was visible, and so they drove back to their earlier position. Something appeared to be moving around the white box, and they returned to the bridge. Ellis bravely climbed the ladder leaning against the bridge and found some loose polythene flapping in the breeze. He secured it with bricks and returned to his colleague in the car.

They surmised that the breeze was causing the movement and the glare from the steelworks was causing the shadows. They decided to wait another 10 or 15 minutes at their original spot and then leave.

The Stocksbridge Bypass (Figgis-West).

The window of the car on Ellis's side was down, and his arm was resting on the door. Suddenly, he was overcome with a feeling of fear. He went cold and could not move his body. He felt that someone was standing next to him with their chest pushed against the open window. He turned his head to the right and saw something by the car. It was the upper half of a man with a 'V' on his chest. The figure vanished and reappeared on the passenger side of the car. Beet screamed and hit Ellis on the arm. Beet had seen a man with piercing eyes, a wizened face, and a pointed nose. He felt that the man was connected to the 1800s. He looked again, and the figure was gone.

Beet was also cold and unable to move. Ellis jumped out of the car and looked for the figure. He even looked under the vehicle but could not find anyone. It would have been impossible for the man to run away in such a short time, and there were no footprints in the mud apart from their own. Ellis got back into the car and drove up Pea Royd Lane, parking at the spot where the security guards had stopped. He radioed for backup, and as they waited, a loud noise was heard from the back of the car.

The officers assumed that someone had run into the vehicle or hit it. They jumped out and heard a series of bangs, like the sound of someone hitting the car with an implement four or five times.

They got back into the car and drove off, meeting their colleagues on the hillside. The other officers made jokes about what the two men had experienced, but a search was made of the area and nothing could be found. Their car was also examined but was found to be unmarked.

The bypass was finally opened to traffic in 1988 and soon acquired a reputation as an accident blackspot.

A bus driver called Neville was walking in the area when he found himself experiencing an icy cold that he likened to opening a freezer door. As he walked up a lane to a field, he felt the hairs standing up on the back of his neck. A sense of oppression was also felt. He then saw what he described as a monk 'racing' around the field.

Others reported seeing a monk-like figure running up the embankment. Sometimes it was caught in the headlights of passing cars. A haulage driver named Melbourne had parked in a trailer park. As he was taking the ropes off his trailer, he suddenly went very cold, even though it was a warm night. He also noticed a musty smell. He glanced up and saw the figure of a monk gliding through the headlights. It then disappeared among the other trailers. He was a regular visitor to the trailer park, and on several other occasions he noticed the musty smell but never saw the figure again. He told his boss about his experience. The man expressed no surprise and remarked, 'Oh, you've seen it as well.'

In July 1992, a couple, David and Judy Simpson, were travelling home one evening after visiting a relative. They were heading towards Wortley when they spotted someone in a field apparently jogging. The figure was running roughly 12 inches above ground level and was heading towards the edge of the field. It had no facial features, and its strangeness was further enhanced by the fact that its arms and legs were distorted and moving in weird directions. It reached the embankment in seconds and rose into the air before falling in front of their car. Mrs. Simpson braked, but there was no sound of impact. Of the figure, there was no sign.

Their sighting was similar to one that had occurred in the autumn of 1987 when Graham Brooke and his son Nigel were jogging near Wortley. It was dusk, and Graham was in front of his son. He saw a figure walking in the centre of the road with his back to the traffic, which Graham thought was a very dangerous thing to do. He stopped and waited in a layby as the figure reached him. It was a man wearing a dark brown cape that was buttoned at the front. He wore gaiters and had a black, featureless face. The clothing looked 17th-century. Nigel had now reached his father and saw the figure too. Both noticed that the man was dragging a large bag and was walking below the present level of the road. The apparition was only visible from just below the knees.

As the man passed them, they noticed a strange musty smell like old newspapers. They were both very afraid and started jogging again. As they did so, the apparition vanished.

A psychic, Elisa Wilkinson, heard of the haunting and decided to investigate it with her daughter, Lesley. They drove to the area where the policemen had their sighting. The bridge was now open to single-lane traffic with temporary traffic lights at each end. It was

11pm, and they decided to get out of the car. The traffic lights started to 'go berserk' as they did so. Elisa then realised that she had left her gloves in the car. As she returned to get them, the door opened by itself. She got her gloves and joined her daughter in climbing the bank to Pea Royd Lane. They then heard footsteps behind them. They turned around and shone their torches in the direction of the footsteps, but could see no one.

The footsteps continued, and the pair then felt as if they were being pushed. They were now under the bridge. It then began to get very warm. It became so hot that they were forced to remove their gloves and scarves and undo their coats. They then discovered that the heat was confined to a circular area about 8ft in diameter. The heat became unbearable, and the mother and daughter decided to leave the bridge and return to the car. It was now 3pm. They had lost three hours, which could not be accounted for.

Elisa sat in the car and attempted to communicate with the apparition. She felt that it was blocking her attempts to reach it. The car had steamed up, and so the window was opened to let in some fresh air. It was at this point that the smell of rotting flesh filled the vehicle. A figure then appeared next to her daughter. It was black and wore a cloak and hood. A sense of evil filled the air as it drifted across the bonnet of the car to the mother's side. It then floated to the boot and then back to the daughter. It then vanished. During its appearance, both mother and daughter experienced numbness in the legs. Elisa fought the feeling, but Lesley became totally paralysed until the figure disappeared. Elisa got out of the car but could see no one. Lesley was now very scared, and they decided to leave the area.

Another psychic, Lucinda June, also claimed to have experienced something while driving on the road. She suddenly felt a presence next to her as she drove through a cutting. Coldness and a smell like musty books filled the air. Hands seemed to be pushing into her back, and then a blackness filled the passenger seat. She started to recite the Lord's Prayer, but this had apparently no effect on the presence. It then vanished. The next day, the medium returned to the same section of road and said that she had managed to contact a monk who had died in tragic circumstances. She was unable to discover more.

Sightings of a monk-like figure continue to this day.

Chapter Two

HELLFIRE CORNER

Dover Castle was founded in the 11th century. The Romans had a fort in the area, and the unique remains of a lighthouse dating from their occupation can still be seen in the castle grounds. For centuries, Dover was regarded as one of the key defences of Britain, and tunnels were dug beneath the castle during the Napoleonic Wars and Second World War in readiness for an invasion from across the Channel. In 1940, the evacuation of Dunkirk was overseen from the tunnels, and British and German planes fought in the skies above the town and port during the Battle of Britain. Dover and the Straits soon became known as Hellfire Corner, as the town was regularly fired upon by German guns from across the Channel. Up to 10,000 buildings in and around the town were damaged by shellfire, and more than 200 civilians were killed. Hundreds more were injured. It was not until September 1944 that the German guns were finally silenced when they fell to British and Canadian troops following the Allied invasion of France.

The church of St. Mary-in-Castro and the adjoining Roman lighthouse are said to

DOVER CASTLE PALACE GATE KEEP

DOVER CASTLE. ST MARY IN THE CASTLE CH. OF PHAROS.

be haunted by a Roman soldier and a monk. The castle is home to a ghostly teenage drummer boy murdered during the Napoleonic period. He is said to haunt the battlements at night, the sounds of his drumming echoing across the deserted castle grounds. One story claims that he was on an errand involving a large sum of money. Two soldiers heard of this and decided to rob him. In the struggle, he was accidentally beheaded by a sword.

The Red Lady haunts the Great Hall. She wears a long, flowing red dress, but who she was in life has been lost to history. She once put in an appearance in the Officers' Mess, which was built in the 19th century. In December 1897, General Sir William Butler was having dinner with some of his officers when a lady in red entered the room looking upset. She insisted to Sir William that there was a fire in the smoking room. A subaltern was sent and found that the chimney was on fire. It was quickly put out,, but the lady insisted that all the rooms be checked. They did, and everything was found to be safe. Sir William then asked the lady who she was. She ignored his question and walked towards the door, vanishing as she neared it.

The next morning, she appeared again. She approached one of the officers by the stables and insisted that he go to his room immediately. The officer ignored her request but was urged by his men to go and look. She then smiled, curtsied, and vanished as she walked across the snow. It was noted that her footsteps left no trace on the ground. The officer went to his room and discovered a fire. It was finally put out but not before causing damage that amounted to over £2,000. It was discovered that the fire was caused by smouldering wood in the roof, a legacy of the chimney fire from the day before. The castle was searched for the mysterious woman, but no trace of her could be found.

The ghost of an English Civil War soldier is said to haunt the tunnels beneath Dover Castle.

DOVER.

DOVER CASTLE.

A figure from the English Civil War haunts the ground floor of the castle. He has been described as wearing a purple cloak, a wide-brimmed hat, and knee-high riding boots. The King's Bed Chamber is also haunted. Visitors have felt a sense of unease there, and the lower half of a figure has been seen walking across the room.

The ghost of an old woman and her black dog haunts Peverell's Tower. A legend states that her little dog was entombed alive in the walls there. This was done as a sacrifice in the hope that it would end the bad luck that had dogged – excuse the pun – the construction of the Norman tower. The dog's howls of terror are still said to be heard from time to time. Some versions of the story claim that the old woman was walled up alongside her dog.

The tunnels beneath the castle are also active. An English Civil War pikeman was seen in the guardroom area, and a soldier dressed in khaki and a nurse have been seen in the hospital. Voices have also been heard in the Dynamo Room.

Leslie Simpson was a tour guide at the castle. He was once showing 20 visitors around the Defence Telecommunications Repeater Station in the tunnels beneath the castle. He noticed that one of the visitors, a woman, was acting strangely. She appeared to be looking at something. She then became alarmed and fell on one knee.

Leslie went to her and asked if she was injured. She said that she was OK. She told him that she had seen a man in a naval uniform at one end of the room. He appeared to be working on some equipment. She thought that he was a member of staff but became alarmed when he started to walk quickly towards the tour group. He reached the barrier and walked right through her! She spun around and saw him vanish through an exit. This was why she had fallen on her knee.

Leslie later took another group around the tunnels but decided to walk ahead to look in the Repeater Station for the apparition. He saw nothing but noticed that a blue door,

One of the Second World War tunnels beneath Dover Castle (Figgis-West).

which led to an annexe, was open. It should have been closed. He then heard a sound from inside that he likened to a mechanical whine combined with an animal noise. He became scared, and the sounds immediately stopped. He never heard the noise again.

A few months later, an Italian tourist saw a figure in a naval uniform near the equipment. He asked Leslie about the man, but no one else had seen him.

Karen Mennie was another guide at the castle. She was taking a tour group around the Repeater Station in the summer of 1993 when she noticed that a father and daughter were acting strangely. The daughter appeared to be talking to an invisible person as the father looked on. The father then left the area, and Karen had to get him to rejoin the rest of the group.

At the end of the tour, the guide told the group that the Repeater Station was supposed to be the most haunted part of the complex. The father then replied that he had seen the ghost. She assumed that he was joking, but he then explained that his daughter had been speaking to the apparition. The father appeared unconcerned by the whole experience, but the daughter appeared to be in shock.

The father claimed that the ghost's name was Bill Billings. He had communicated with the father and said that he was a postal telecommunications officer from Canterbury. He had been killed assembling some amplifier racks. Attempts were made to see if this information was correct, but it was found that the local military records for the war years were not complete.

Another interesting experience was recounted by two American tourists. They had been visiting the castle and tunnels and commented on the sound effects used during the tour. They were especially impressed with the sounds used around the area of St. John's Tower.

The groans and shrieks had been particularly effective, they said. The tour guide explained that no sound effects were used in the castle or tunnels. After the couple had left, the area was searched in case someone had been injured and was responsible for the cries heard by the Americans. No one was found.

Philip Wyborn-Brown, another member of staff, is a sceptic and attributes much of the phenomena to natural causes such as draughts and shadows cast by the light. However, even he had a strange experience in the castle. He was checking the building one evening to ensure that all the tourists had left. As he locked up, he saw a figure pass the Great Hall and walk into the King's Bed Chamber. He dismisses the idea that it could have been a ghost and believes it was caused by a shadow.

In 1991, the Thanet Psychic and Paranormal Research Unit and the Association for the Scientific Study of Anomalous Phenomena conducted a series of night vigils in the castle.

On October 12, one of the investigators was in a passageway in the castle. He heard a noise like a wooden door slamming. The time was 11.22pm.

At 2.20am, two other members of the team were on the second floor of the keep. A loud bang was heard from behind a locked door that led to the west stairwell. The door was opened, but nothing could be found to account for the noise. The door was again locked, and the two investigators walked away. As they did so, the door shook for several seconds.

Two other members were staying in the St. John's Tower area when they saw a shadowy figure moving down a stairwell. One of the team called out, and the figure turned and walked quickly back up the stairs. They assumed that it was another member of the team,

Interior of Castle Keep, Dover.

The King's Bed Chamber (Figgis-West).

The King's Bed Chamber (Figgis-West).

but when they asked him, he explained that he had been at the other end of the passageway at the time of the sighting.

The same two investigators heard the sound of a heavy wooden door being shut at 3.30am and then again just over an hour later. This time, the sound was recorded on tape. Other members of the team also heard doors slamming.

It was decided to train a camera on the wooden doors in the keep, which had been seen shaking. It was a wise decision, as the film captured both doors being violently shaken for several seconds. One of the investigators cried out, 'We've got it!' and the shaking stopped. A search was made of the area, but nothing could be found to account for what had been witnessed.

Other sounds were heard in St. John's Tower during the vigil. One was likened to the dropping of a pebble onto the wooden stairs. Four members of the team heard this.

A second vigil was held on November 30. A tape recorder was left on in the keep. The sounds of it being interfered with were recorded. The smell of perfume was noted in the area, and in the basement, two loud bangs were heard.

Members of the ITV series *Strange But True* were filming an episode in the castle, and a psychic, Michael Bromley, was filmed in the tunnels trying to contact the ghosts there. He mentioned the name Helen in the Repeater Station, but Clive Boreham of English Heritage was unimpressed as no women were historically associated with that area. A few days after the TV crew had departed, an Australian tourist, Annie Sallows, was visiting the castle and tunnels. She suddenly saw an apparition running up to her. She described him as blonde and said that he was wearing a navy blue uniform. He spoke to her and said that his name was Samuel. He was quite agitated and kept asking where Helen was. Clive Boreham was astonished when the tourist told him as she had not been aware of what the medium had said only a few days before. He admitted that this experience had now left him with an open mind.

Chapter Three

MOST CURIOUS TALES

BLACK SHUCK

East Anglia has long been known as the haunt of a ghostly dog known as Black Shuck. He is usually described as being a very large black dog with blazing red eyes. His name may derive from the Old English word 'scucca,' meaning demon, or possibly from the local word 'shucky,' meaning 'shaggy' or 'hairy'.

It is said that to see him is an omen of impending disaster or even death, although not always. An acquaintance of mine, a bookseller, once saw a very large black dog – described by him as being the size of a pony – while driving down a Suffolk lane near Saxmundham. He suffered no ill effects and is still very much alive.

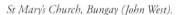

St Mary's Church, Bungay (John West).

A ſtraunge,

and terrible Wunder wrougbt
very late in the parish Churcb
of Bongay, a Tovvn of no great di-
ſtance from the citie of Norvvicb, name-
ly the fourth of this Auguſt, in ỹ yeere of
our Lord 1577. in a great tempeſt of violent raine, lightning, and thunder, the
like wherof hath bén ſel-
dome ſeene.

With the apperance of an horrible ſha-
ped thing, ſenſibly perceiued of the
people then and there
aſſembled.

Drawen into a plain method according to the written coppie.
by Abraham Fleming.

Title page of Rev. Abraham Fleming's account of the appearance of the ghostly black dog.

On August 4, 1577, Shuck is alleged to have entered St. Mary's Church in the Suffolk town of Bungay during a violent storm. He ran down the aisle, attacking several members of the congregation.

An old verse records:

All down the church in midst of fire, the hellish monster flew
And, passing onward to the quire, he many people slew.

Shuck's appearance was described in *A Straunge and Terrible Wunder* by the Rev Abraham Fleming in 1577: 'This black dog, or the divel in such a linenesse (God hee knoweth al who worketh all,) runing all along down the body of the church with great swiftnesse, and incredible haste, among the people, in a visible fourm and shape, passed between two persons, as they were kneeling uppon their knees, and occupied in prayer as it seemed, wrung the necks of them bothe at one instant clene backward, in somuch that even at a moment where they kneeled, they strangely dyed.'

It should be noted that the churchwarden's account book from the time does indeed mention the storm. The parish register also records the deaths of two men in the belfry. However, neither mentions a dog nor attributes the storm or the deaths to the work of the Devil.

Some modern scholars attribute the whole mysterious event to a lightning strike. And did it coincide with the appearance of a terrified dog seeking shelter from the storm? Sixteenth-century Britain was a land of superstition, with belief in witchcraft and Satanic forces widespread. With this in mind, it is hardly surprising that the violent storm, the deaths of the two men, and the sudden appearance of a dog would all be blamed on the Devil.

Whatever the explanation, scratch marks on the inside of the north door are still pointed out as evidence of Shuck's visit.

THE HAPPISBURGH SMUGGLER

Crossing the border into Norfolk and travelling north along the coast will eventually take you to the shoreline below the village of Happisburgh, the reputed haunt of a terrifying apparition. Over the years, people have claimed to have witnessed a figure with no legs, its head hanging down its back by a strip of flesh. It was first seen in 1765 by two farmers who were making their way home one night along Whimpwell Street. It was reported to be wearing sailor's clothes and appeared to be holding a sack to its chest. Upon reaching a well, it dropped the sack and vanished. The well was later searched, and the remains of a dismembered man were found hidden in two sacks. A pistol was also found with the corpse. It was surmised that he may have been a smuggler and had been murdered by his

The ghost of a murdered smuggler is said to haunt Happisburgh.

colleagues after some dispute over booty. This belief was confirmed a few weeks later when signs of the sailor's murder were found by locals at nearby Cart Gap. A pistol matching the one discovered with the body was picked up, along with several gold coins. There were broken whisky bottles strewn about, and the sand was stained with dried blood.

The spectre of the murdered man apparently still haunts the area. The well has long gone, but some still claim to hear strange moans and groans emanating from the spot. Apparently, the ideal time to see the ghost is on moonlit nights.

THERE IS A FUTURE STATE

York Minster, one of Britain's most beautiful buildings, has stood for centuries, a towering testament to man's faith in God and all His works.

It is hardly surprising to learn that the Minster is said to be haunted. One interesting story can be found in *Accredited Ghost Stories* (1823) by T.M. Jarvis. It concerns the spirit of a man who came back with a message of hope and reassurance: 'It is not many years ago since Mr. B. L. accompanied some friends on a visit to York Cathedral. The party was numerous, and amongst them were a gentleman and his two daughters. Mr. B. L. was with the eldest of these ladies, exploring the curiosities of the building, rather at a distance from the rest of their companions. On turning from the monument to which their attention had been directed, an officer in a naval uniform was observed advancing towards them. It

was rather an unusual circumstance to encounter a person thus accoutred in a place so far distant from the sea and of so unmilitary a character. Mr. B. L. was on the point of making a trivial observation on the subject to his companion when, on turning his eyes towards her and pointing out the approaching stranger to her notice, he saw an immediate paleness spread over her face, and her countenance became agitated by the force of the powerful and contending emotions which were suddenly excited by his presence.

'As the stranger drew more near and his figure and his features gradually became more distinctly visible through the evening gloom and the dim religious light of the cathedral, the lady's distress was evidently increased. She leant on the arm of Mr. B. L. with the weight of one who was painfully afflicted and felt the necessity of support. Shocked at the oppression which he witnessed but wholly ignorant of the cause, Mr. B. L. called to entreat the assistance of her sister. The figure in the naval uniform was now immediately before them. The eyes of the lady were fixed upon him with a gaze of silent and motionless surprise and a painful intensity of feeling; her lips were colourless and apart, and her breath passed heavily from the full and overburdened heart. The form was close upon them; it approached her side; it paused but for an instant; as quick as thought, a low and scarcely audible voice whispered in her ear; "There is a future state."

The figure then moved off and was soon lost from view. A search was made, but no trace of the man could be found. The weeping daughter then spoke: 'I have seen the spirit, and I have heard the voice of a brother, who exists no longer; he has perished at sea. We had agreed that the one who died the first should reappear to the survivor, if it were possible, to clear up or to confirm the religious doubts which existed in both our minds.'

In due course, word was received that the brother had indeed passed away. His death had happened at the same moment he had been seen by Mr. B. L. and the lady.

THE RETURN OF FREDDY JACKSON

In 1919, the men and women from HMS *Daedalus*, a training facility, were gathered together at RAF Cranwell for a squadron group photograph before being disbanded.

Sir Victor Goddard, KCB, CBE, wrote of the photograph in his book *Flight Towards Reality*: 'It shows a group of airmen, airwomen, and officers, some hundreds of them, in various uniforms, RNAS and Army, RFC and RAF, ATS and Women's Naval Service, all my contemporaries and one my friend. The photograph is typical of all the chaos of transition from the two old separate Services, into the Royal Air Force, which then was still quite new and unfamiliar. The RAF had not by then been lifted up into its corporate consciousness of entity and destiny.

'The Squadron, of which the photograph was taken, had no future; it was to be disbanded, and almost everyone then photographed was also in transition back to that less authoritarian life which they called "Civvy Street".

'But one was otherwise.

'When the group photograph was put up on the noticeboard so that those who wanted copies could write their names below, those who scanned the photograph identifying friends then saw – or they were prompted then to see – the face of Freddy Jackson, air mechanic, in the topmost row. Capless and smiling, his face being partly hidden by

Did the ghost of Freddy Jackson appear in this photograph?

another, his expression seemed to say, "My goodness me – I nearly failed to make it! … They didn't wait, or leave a place for me, the blighters!"

'Well, there he was, and no mistake, although a little fainter than the rest. Indeed, he looked as though he was not altogether there; not really with the group, for he alone was capless, smiling, all the rest were serious and set and wearing service caps. Most had not long returned from Church Parade and marching in a military funeral. For Freddy Jackson had, upon that very spot – the Squadron tarmac – three days before, walked heedlessly into the whirling propeller of an aeroplane. He had been killed stone dead instantly. He, evidently, was still quite unaware of it.

There had been no hanky-panky in the dark room. The negative was scrutinised for faking and was found to be untouched.'

Sceptics claim that the photograph is just another example of double exposure and can be put down to a case of mistaken identity. However, they choose to ignore a very simple and important fact – the people in the photograph swore that they recognised the face as being that of Freddy Jackson. And why is the ghostly figure the only one without a cap if it was simply a double exposure?

Freddy had been buried on the very day that his former colleagues found themselves standing before the official photographer for a final squadron portrait. So did a dead man make one last journey to rejoin his friends and colleagues before they all went their separate ways?

THE GHOST IN THE LIBRARY

On December 5, 1891, a photograph was taken that many still claim provides clear evidence of life after death. The photographer, Sybell Corbet, had decided to take some pictures of Combermere Abbey in Cheshire, the former home of the late Lord Combermere. Combermere had recently died in a carriage accident, and almost all of the household and family were away attending his funeral at the time.

One of the photographs featured the library. The picture was taken at 2pm, with the exposure of the plate lasting an hour. Miss Corbet did not stay in the room for the whole of this period.

She developed the plate herself and was amazed to see a transparent figure, only visible from the waist up, sitting in Combermere's favourite high-backed chair. The plate was shown to close relatives of the deceased, and all agreed that the figure was Lord Combermere. Miss Corbet also confirmed that the plate had not been used before, thereby ruling out the possibility of an earlier photographic image accidentally appearing on the plate.

She was also adamant that neither of the two remaining staff had entered the room during the exposure. This was also confirmed by the butler, one of the remaining staff. The case was investigated by Professor William Barrett and Gordon Salt of the Society for

THE COMBERMERE GHOST.
See partially built up figure in chair on left.

Psychical Research. They concluded that the ghost was a case of double exposure. Barrett wrote, 'I believe that one of the servants came into the room, sat down in the chair, crossed his legs and then uncrossed them, looked down for a moment, and then at the camera, saw that he was being taken, so got up and went away, having been in the chair about 20 to 30 seconds. This will give the ghost of an apparently older man from a young man, with no legs and a semi-transparent face, etc.'

It must be said that many people still disagree with Barrett's verdict. It has been pointed out that the indoor servants at the mansion wore livery, unlike the figure in the chair. Lord Combermere's daughter-in-law also stated that the figure did not resemble any of the servants in the house. She also confirmed that all of the outdoor servants were attending the funeral, thereby ruling out the possibility of any of them entering the house at the time the plate was being exposed. We must also not forget that Lord Combermere's close relatives were all convinced that the figure was him.

I remain open-minded about this particular spirit photograph. However, it is interesting to note that the figure appeared in the chair at the exact moment Lord Combermere was being buried.

THE PHANTOM PRIEST

This photograph dates from 1940 and was taken by a solicitor in St. Nicholas' Church, Arundel, Sussex. The church stands on the site of a Norman priory and has a reputation

Was a ghostly figure captured in this photograph taken in Arundel Church?

for being haunted. The figure of a nun supposedly haunts the bell tower, and a woman in blue has been seen standing near the altar.

Little is known about the exact circumstances behind the photograph, and even the name of the solicitor is now unfortunately lost to history. It is said that the image shows a transparent priest-like figure standing before the altar. However, a computer analysis made in the 1980s claims to have found that the image was simply 'a multiple exposure of a woman ascending the altar steps with a taper and lighting one of the altar candles'.

The fact that we have so little information regarding the background of this photograph makes the computer analysis very hard to refute. It must be said that the apparition does appear to be dressed in female clothing, and a streak of light to the left of the figure could be due to a lighted taper as the woman walked up the steps to the altar. However, as already stated, the church is supposedly haunted by two female phantoms. So did the solicitor capture a ghost after all?

THE GHOST SHIP

In 1743, William John Lewis was ploughing his fields on his farm at Peibio on the island of Anglesey. He looked up and saw a two-masted sailboat coming towards him from the direction of the mountains. It was about a quarter of a mile from the ground, and the farmer could clearly see its sails and pennants flying. He rushed to get his wife, and when they returned, the ship, its sails now neatly furled, was heading back to the mountains, a flock of birds mobbing it as it neared them. When later questioned about the apparition, it emerged that the farmer had seen these aerial ships before. He went on to explain that they appeared to him at ten-year intervals.

THE GLAMORGAN VAMPIRE

In Glamorgan, Wales, there was a very old farmhouse that was filled with ancient furniture. In the 18th century, a dissenting minister was preaching in the area. He was allowed to stay in the house and was given the best bedroom. He would get up early in the morning to write his sermons and decided on this occasion to sit in an old wooden chair next to the window as he wrote. When he got up, he noticed that his hand was bleeding badly and that there was a pool of blood beneath the chair. He had experienced no pain, but he did notice what appeared to be a set of teeth marks on the back of his hand.

At breakfast, he told his host of his injury and said that he thought there was a nail sticking out of the chair. His hostess replied that others had complained of being scratched in the chair, although their injuries had usually been to the palm rather than the back of the hand. Two days later, the minister was asleep in his bed when he was awoken by a sharp pain in his left side, as if a dog was gnawing at his flesh. He found teeth marks on his chest and later discovered similar bites on his horse when he collected it from the stable.

He sought out the hostess and said, 'Madam, you may not know it, but I believe a vampire frequents this house. The dead man who owned the furniture comes to suck the blood from intruders, even from the grey mare in your stable. And probably he is not pleasantly disposed towards ministers of the gospels.'

The vampire strikes!

The lady replied that he was right and admitted that it happened to other ministers but never to their horses. The attack was forgotten, but in 1850, a dignitary of the Church of England was staying in the farmhouse and was bitten in the leg and arm. It was decided to sell all the ancient furniture and effects, and from then on, nothing more was heard from the vampire.

THE THING ON THE MOUNTAIN

Showell Styles, in his book *The Mountains of North Wales,* writes of a very strange experience when climbing in the Welsh mountains. He was 3,000ft up Bwlch y Ddwy-Glyder when he noticed below him what he assumed was a walker dressed in brown coming up the slope. He then realised that it was too big to be human. It was also moving too swiftly up the loose stones and boulders. It looked more like a bear and was transparent. The thing was making a roaring or rushing noise as it moved to the crest of the pass just 20 yards below where he was sitting, disappearing from view as it went over the edge. On closer inspection, the thing was a whirling mass of dried grass that appeared to be six or seven feet in diameter. There was not the slightest breath of wind on the ridge or mountain, and he was at a loss to explain what could have caused the phenomenon.

THE SCREAM

Thomas Davies of Rhyl was employed as a fox controller by farmers in the Llandudno area. One evening, he found a vixen's den in Gloddaeth Wood. The mother and her cubs were still inside, and he decided to hide in a nearby old oak tree and wait for the vixen to emerge. Suddenly, he heard a terrible scream coming from the direction of the sea. The scream came again, only this time it was much closer and sounded more anguished. A third scream came, and he now realised, to his horror, that it was close by. The cry came again, and Davies saw 'a nude being with eyes burning like fire.' The creature was beneath him, crouching, standing erect, and then crouching again as it gazed up at him. It stayed there for hours, but at the first light of dawn and the crow of a cock, it vanished.

Chapter Four

THE BROWN LADY OF
RAYNHAM HALL

Raynham Hall, owned by the Townshend family, has long been regarded as one of the finest country houses in Norfolk. A large part of the hall dates back to the 17th century and has a wealth of architectural wonders, including painted ceilings and elaborately carved chimney pieces by William Kent. The house can also boast several ghosts.

The ill-fated Duke of Monmouth supposedly haunts one of the bedrooms; a phantom dog has been heard running up and down the corridors; and a little girl in a dress has been seen in the Stone Parlour.

Raynham Hall has one other ghostly resident, Dorothy Walpole, and she has been the subject of fierce debate ever since her ghost was allegedly captured on camera in the 1930s.

No. J. & S. 7840   RAYNHAM HALL.

The Duke of Monmouth is said to haunt the hall.

Dorothy was the sister of Robert Walpole, the first prime minister of Great Britain. In 1713, she married Charles Townshend and moved into the Raynham family home. The marriage proved less than a success, and Dorothy found herself accused of having an affair behind her husband's back. Townshend forced her to remain at the hall for the rest of her life. She died of smallpox in 1726.

The Prince Regent, later George IV, claimed to have seen Dorothy's ghost

Dorothy Walpole.

The Prince Regent vowed never to return to Raynham Hall after seeing the ghost of the Brown Lady.

when he was a guest at the hall. He was staying in the Green Velvet State Bedchamber but decided to leave after seeing the phantom. He told his guests that he would ' not pass another hour in this accursed house, for I have seen what I hope to God I may never see again.' He claimed to have witnessed the figure of 'a little lady all dressed in brown with dishevelled hair and a face of ashy paleness.'

The next recorded sighting of the ghost was during Christmas celebrations in 1835. A lady wearing a brown dress was seen in a corridor by Colonel Loftus and another guest named Hawkins. It was again seen by Loftus the following night. He later reported that the figure had a glowing face and appeared eyeless.

Reports of these appearances led to Captain Frederick Marryat, a friend of Charles Dickens, visiting the hall in 1836. Marryat was convinced that the ghost was a hoax and asked to spend the night in the bedroom, where the Brown Lady was often said to appear. However, other sources claim that his visit took place several years later.

In 1917, his daughter Florence wrote of what happened: 'He took possession of the room in which the portrait of the apparition hung, and in which she had been often seen, and slept each night with a loaded revolver under his pillow. For two days, however, he saw nothing, and the third was to be the limit of his stay. On the third night, however, two young men (nephews of the baronet) knocked at his door as he was undressing to go to bed and asked him to step over to their room (which was at the other end of the corridor) and give them his opinion on a new gun that had just arrived from London. My father was in his shirt and trousers, but as the hour was late and everybody had retired to rest except themselves, he prepared to accompany them as he was. As they were leaving the room, he caught up his revolver, "in case you meet the Brown Lady", he said, laughing. When the inspection of the gun was over, the young men, in the same spirit, declared they would accompany my father back again, "in case you meet the Brown Lady", they repeated, laughing also. The three gentlemen, therefore, returned in company.

'The corridor was long and dark, for the lights had been extinguished, but as they reached the middle of it, they saw the glimmer of a lamp coming towards them from the other end. "One of the ladies going to visit the nurseries," whispered the young Townshends to my father. Now the bedroom doors in that corridor faced each other, and each room had a double door with a space between, as is the case in many old-fashioned houses. My father, as I have said, was in shirt and trousers only, and his native modesty made him feel uncomfortable, so he slipped within one of the outer doors (his friends following his example) in order to conceal himself until the lady should have passed by.

'I have heard him describe how he watched her approaching nearer and nearer, through the chink of the door, until, as she was close enough for him to distinguish the colours and style of her costume, he recognised the figure as the facsimile of the portrait of "The Brown Lady". He had his finger on the trigger of his revolver and was about to demand it to stop and give the reason for its presence there when the figure halted of its own accord before the door behind which he stood and, holding the lighted lamp she carried to her features, grinned in a malicious and diabolical manner at him. This act so infuriated my father, who was anything but lamb-like in disposition, that he sprang into the corridor with a bound and discharged the revolver right in her face. The figure instantly disappeared – the figure

The Brown Lady of Raynham Hall, one of the most famous ghost photographs of the 20th century.

at which for several minutes three men had been looking together – and the bullet passed through the outer door of the room on the opposite side of the corridor and lodged in the panel of the inner one. My father never attempted again to interfere with "The Brown Lady of Raynham."

The Brown Lady appeared to remain quiet until 1926, when she was seen on a staircase by the son of Lady Townshend. It was also witnessed at the same time by his friend. They identified the ghost by comparing her to a portrait of Dorothy Walpole that was hanging in the so-called Haunted Room.

Ten years were to pass before she was seen again. It was September 19, 1936, and Captain Hubert C. Provand, a photographer working for *Country Life* magazine, and his

Harry Price was impressed by the photograph of the Brown Lady.

assistant, Indre Shira, were at the hall to take photographs for a feature. It was decided to photograph the main staircase. Shira described what happened next: 'Captain Provand took one photograph while I flashed the light. He was focusing for another exposure; I was standing by his side just behind the camera with the flashlight pistol in my hand, looking directly up the staircase. All at once, I detected an ethereal, veiled form coming slowly down the stairs. Rather excitedly, I called out sharply, "Quick, quick, there's something." I pressed the trigger of the flashlight pistol. After the flash and on closing the shutter, Captain Provand removed the focusing cloth from his head and, turning to me, said, "What's all the excitement about?"

Later, when the negative was developed, the image of the ghost was revealed. The account of their experience, including the photograph of the apparition, was published in *Country Life* on December 26, 1936. The picture went global, and even today it is still hailed as one of the greatest examples of spirit photography on record.

Harry Price, the noted paranormal investigator and author, interviewed Provand and Shira and reflected, 'I will say at once I was impressed. I was told a perfectly simple story: Mr. Indre Shira saw the apparition descending the stairs at the precise moment when Captain Provand's head was under the black cloth. A shout – and the cap was off and the flashbulb fired, with the results which we now see. I could not shake their story, and I had no right to disbelieve them. Only collusion between the two men would account for the ghost if it is a fake. The negative is entirely innocent of any faking.'

In recent years, the photograph has been re-examined, and serious doubts have been raised regarding its authenticity. It is claimed that the picture shows evidence of double exposure, especially on the stair treads and bannisters. Some have even gone so far as to state that the image is a deliberate hoax orchestrated by Provand and Shira to gain notoriety. They suggest that the figure resembles a statue of the Virgin Mary and believe that it was added to the original negative after the pair had left the hall.

Supporters of the photograph reject this and say that independent researchers at the time regarded the negative as genuine and certainly not the product of any trickery. They also cite a declaration from a chemist, Mr. Jones, who saw the negative being fixed: 'I saw the negative of the Oak [sic] staircase at Raynham Hall in the hypo bath in your dark room immediately after it had been taken by Captain Provand from the developer. I am satisfied that the ethereal figure on the staircase was there when the film was being fixed.'

So is the photograph a fake or a genuine example of spirit photography, and is Raynham Hall really haunted by the unhappy spirit of Dorothy Walpole? You decide!

Chapter Five

THE SINKING OF THE TITANIC:
A TRAGEDY FORESEEN?

On a cold night in April 1912, the *Titanic* hit an iceberg and sank with the loss of over 1,500 lives. At the time, the ship was thought by many to be unsinkable, and the news that it had gone down in less than three hours after the collision seemed almost impossible to believe. Some sought comfort in the assurance that no one could have possibly foreseen the disaster, but even this belief was challenged when it emerged that a large number of people had apparent premonitions of the sinking before that fateful night. Stories of passengers suddenly cancelling their tickers due to a sense of foreboding, crew members leaving the ship without explanation, and relatives sensing the passing of their loved ones at the very time they were struggling for survival in the icy waters of the Atlantic all soon emerged in print.

The Titanic under construction in Belfast.

So is it really possible to see into the future, and could the loss of the *Titanic* have been averted if these apparent psychic warnings had been given to the officials of White Star Line, the owners of the liner?

Or did fate decree that the *Titanic* was destined to sink on that terrible night over a century ago?

FUTILITY

In 1898, Morgan Robertson wrote a novel entitled *Futility* (later republished as *The Wreck of the Titan*). The story concerned a fictional liner called the *Titan*, which was described as being the largest ship afloat. The ship did not have enough lifeboats for all on board but was described as being unsinkable. Some 14 years later, the real-life *Titanic*, which was the largest ship afloat, did not have enough lifeboats for the passengers and crew but was thought by many to be unsinkable. The *Titan* was 45,000 tons and 800ft long, with a triple-screw propeller. The *Titanic* was 46,000 tons and 882ft long, with a triple-screw propeller. The *Titan*'s maiden voyage took place in April. The *Titanic* sailed on April 10. Travelling at 25 knots, the *Titan* struck an iceberg on her starboard side on an April night in the North Atlantic, 400 nautical miles from Newfoundland, and sank with most of her passengers and crew. Travelling at 22.5 knots, the *Titanic* struck an iceberg on the starboard side at 11.40pm on April 14, 1912, in the North Atlantic, 400 nautical miles from Newfoundland, with the loss of over 1,500 passengers and crew.

Mr. Robertson always denied that his novel was a premonition of the *Titanic* disaster, claiming that it was based on his knowledge of the sea and current shipbuilding trends. Nevertheless, the similarities between the fictional *Titan* and the real-life *Titanic* are startling, even if they are just coincidences.

THE GYPSY

In 1911, an officer with the ship *George Washington* was visiting Bremerhaven, in Germany. He was there with his wife and two daughters. They decided to visit a gypsy camp to have their palms read by an elderly woman. The officer laughed as she looked at his palm, but then noticed a strange look on the gypsy's face. 'You may laugh,' the woman said. 'They always do laugh, but on the sea lies your work, and next year the greatest ship in the world will sink – sink!'

The officer laughed again as the woman cried, thrusting his hand aside. 'I have told you too much! I see too much! Sadness – death – sinking – sinking!'

The family left the tent highly amused by her predictions. The officer was not destined to sail on the *Titanic*, but her prediction that next year the 'greatest ship in the world will sink' was striking, to say the least.

RMS Titanic leaving Belfast for her sea trials on April 2, 1912.

I SHALL GO DOWN WITH HER

The early part of 1912 saw Captain E.J. Smith of the *Olympic* (*Titanic*'s older sister ship) host a get-together of his officers and their wives. It was pointed out that a prophecy had been published the previous year, which claimed that the largest ship in the world would sink the following spring with great loss of life. Captain Smith, soon to be transferred to the *Titanic*, commented, 'Well, if the largest liner in the world goes down, I shall go down with her.'

The wife of an officer, hearing Captain Smith's comments, suddenly became filled with foreboding as her husband was to sail on the *Titanic*. Her fears were sadly justified, as her husband was to join Captain Smith in a watery grave.

Captain Edward J. Smith.

RMS Titanic in Southhampton Dock.

THE DREAM

It was late March 1912, and a young farmer in Athenry, Ireland, had decided to emigrate to the USA. He chose the *Titanic* and booked a place in steerage. His mother dreamed on three successive nights that the *Titanic* would sink in the mid-Atlantic with all on board. She begged her son to cancel the trip, which he finally did. Sadly, we do not know the names of the son and mother, as they were withheld by the press at the time to ensure their privacy.

I KNEW ALL ALONG HE WOULD BE SAFE

Arthur Lewis joined the *Titanic* as a steward. He asked his wife to sew the White Star insignia on his cap. As she was doing this, the star 'fell all to pieces.' Mrs. Lewis felt this was a bad omen, but her concerns were dismissed by her husband. He joined the *Titanic* the next day.

Mr. Lewis was lucky enough to man one of the lifeboats and so survived. It was not until April 20 that his wife was told he was alive. However, she revealed that she had been unconcerned by the delay in learning of his fate because 'I knew all along he would be safe. A voice kept telling me he would be all right.'

WE SHALL NEVER SEE OUR CHILDREN AGAIN

On April 9, 1912, a 'well-known solicitor' in London had a strange encounter in his office: 'Barely a day before the *Titanic* sailed, a wealthy businessman came to me and considerably surprised me by asking if I could consent to be a guardian to his two little boys. I naturally asked him what he meant, and he replied, "Tomorrow, I and my wife are sailing on *Titanic*. I cannot tell why, but I feel that something is going to happen and that we shall never see our children again."'

After the disaster, the solicitor told reporters, 'Up to the present, neither his name nor that of his wife appear among the saved.' The solicitor declined to name the businessman to ensure his client's privacy. It was never revealed if the man or his wife survived the sinking.

TRUE TILL DEATH

Three days before the *Titanic* left Southampton, a member of the crew and his wife recorded themselves singing together. The crewman sang 'True Till Death' and the wife sang 'Only To See Her Face Again.' The crewman did not survive the sinking. His widow vowed never to play the recording again.

IF YOU EVER FIND MY BODY

Peter C. Hanson and his wife Jennie were returning home to Racine, Wisconsin, after a trip to Denmark, where they had been visiting Mr. Hanson's family.

Before the outward journey, Mrs. Hanson confided in her brother, Thomas Howard, that she dreaded the visit: "I have a feeling that I will never return alive. I just know the boat will sink or something awful will happen to me either going over or coming back.' She even described the clothes that she wanted to be buried in and what flowers should be placed on her coffin. The brother laughed it off and bid her farewell.

The time finally came for the return journey, and the couple, along with Mr. Hanson's brother Henry, decided to book three places on the *Titanic*. As the ship sank, Peter Hanson placed his wife into a lifeboat with the words, 'Jennie, you had better go so that there will be one of us to tell the story back home.' Her husband and brother-in-law went down with the ship.

IT IS DOOMED!

Emma Bucknell of Philadelphia had been staying in Europe for the winter. She was booked to return home on the *Titanic* when it visited Cherbourg. A friend, Mrs. J. J. Brown – later known as the 'Unsinkable Molly Brown' – was also returning home with her. Mrs. Bucknell was still in Paris when she was filled with foreboding. 'I'm deathly afraid to go aboard that ship', she told her friend. 'I feel sure something terrible is going to happen.'

Despite Mrs. Bucknell's fear, the pair continued to Cherbourg. It was April 10, and they found themselves on the tender, which was due to take them to the ship. Mrs. Bucknell suddenly grabbed her friend's arm and said, 'Oh, I dread, I really dread going aboard that ship. It is doomed. I feel it! I know it!'

Molly Brown.

Titanic's First Class gymnasium.

Mrs. Brown ignored the warnings, and Mrs. Bucknell reluctantly agreed to board the liner. Her unease never left her, and on the evening of April 14, she found herself in the first-class dining room with her friend and Dr. Arthur Brewe, a physician from Philadelphia who was returning home from Italy. Mrs. Bucknell again voiced her concerns: 'I felt nervous when we boarded at Cherbourg, and I still feel that way. I don't know what it is, but ever since I got on this ship, I've felt premonitions of disaster.'

Mrs. Brown again dismissed her unease, saying, 'Well, I'm not going to lose any sleep over your premonitions. In fact, that's where I'll be going very soon – to sleep. It's too cold to do anything else.'

The two ladies were both in their rooms when the ship hit the iceberg. Encountering each other on the dock, Mrs. Bucknell said to Mrs. Brown, 'Didn't I tell you? I knew it!'

Both survived the sinking, having found a place in the lifeboats. Dr. Brewe was not so lucky. He perished with the ship.

I CAN SEE HUNDREDS OF PEOPLE STRUGGLING IN THE ICY WATER

On April 10, Jack and Blanche Marshall, their daughters, friends, and servants were watching the *Titanic* steaming by their home, which overlooked the Solent.

The group was shocked when Blanche suddenly grabbed her husband's arm and cried, 'That ship is going to sink before it reaches America!' Her husband tried to calm her, but this only made her more upset. Assurances from her friends that the *Titanic* was unsinkable only made matters worse. 'Don't stand there staring at me!', she shouted. 'Do something! You fools, I can see hundreds of people struggling in the icy water. Are you so blind that you are going to let them drown?'

The subject of the *Titanic* was left unmentioned after this outburst. Five days later, word arrived that she had sunk.

The *Titanic* premonition was not destined to be Mrs. Marshall's only glimpse into the future.

In 1915, Mrs. Marshall and her husband were booked to sail on the *Lusitania* on May 1. Upon seeing the tickets on the mantelpiece, Mrs. Marshall suddenly told her husband, 'The *Lusitania* is going to sink on that voyage. Jack, change the reservations!' He reluctantly agreed and booked an earlier passage that sailed some three weeks earlier. It was still the *Lusitania*! However, this time Mrs. Marshall was unconcerned, saying, 'Oh, that's all right, the *Lusitania* is not going to sink until the voyage we were going on. I suppose she will be torpedoed, as it is still too warm for icebergs. Poor things, I feel so sorry for them! However, there is nothing we can do about it in wartime.'

The *Lusitania* was torpedoed on May 7 by a German U-boat. She sank with the loss of 1,198 lives.

Titanic's First Class Turkish Baths.

ON ITS FIRST VOYAGE

It was March 1912, and Helen E. Bell was reading the *Daily Mail* after finishing her breakfast. She was looking at an article on the *Titanic* by Hamilton Fyfe, in which he described the ship's imminent departure from the Belfast docks, 'As I read, a picture suddenly formed between myself and the paper, showing a night scene with what I took to be jagged and pointed rocks, with the hull of a boat standing out of the water. With the picture came a voice, clear and distinct, that said, "This will be on its first voyage." I instantly asked, "Why? What is the matter with the boat?" The voice replied, "Nothing; that is all right, but it will be on its first voyage."'

Miss Bell felt dismayed but got no further images or messages. The picture she saw was described by her as appearing 'to be about five by four inches in size and resembled in its various gradations of light and shade an old steel engraving. I should have called it a gem had I seen it on exhibition.'

Miss Bell was later asked by friends why, after the vision, she had not tried to warn the press. She replied, 'Where is the newspaper that would have printed it?'

WHATEVER'S GOING TO HAPPEN, I FEEL SURE, WILL HAPPEN IN THE NIGHT

Benjamin Hart decided to emigrate to Canada with his wife Esther and their seven-year-old daughter Eva. Mrs. Hart was filled with dismay upon hearing this, saying she was 'certain that the whole plan would bring only unhappiness.' She begged her husband several times to abandon his desire to leave England, but he refused. His wife declined to mention the subject again but continued to have a sense of impending disaster. The family was originally destined to sail on the ship *Philadelphia*, but the voyage was cancelled due to a coal strike. Mrs. Hart took comfort in this and believed that fate would prevent them from sailing on another ship.

Sadly, her relief was short-lived, as a few days later a letter arrived giving the family the chance to sail on the *Titanic*. Mr. Hart told his wife, 'I know you haven't wanted to go up to now, but surely now that you know you're going on this wonderful ship, the chance of a lifetime, surely you've overcome all your fears.'

His wife was still far from happy. 'Oh, no. I feel even worse about it than I did before.' Weeping, she then asked her husband if the *Titanic* was said to be unsinkable. He replied that it was. This distressed her even more. 'That is flying in the face of God, and now, at last, I know why I am so afraid. That ship will never get to the other side of the Atlantic.'

The fateful day arrived when the couple and their daughter, Eva, were due to join the ship. Mrs. Hart again pleaded with her husband not to board her but was met with an angry reply that he would travel on the ship alone if need be. He added that she and their

Benjamin, Eva and Esther Hart. Esther was convinced that the Titanic was in danger.

child could go home to her mother and join him on a later voyage. Mrs. Hart reluctantly backed down and made her way on board.

Upon reaching the cabin, Mrs. Hart told her husband that she would sleep during the day and stay up at night 'because whatever's going to happen, I feel sure, will happen in the night.'

Mrs. Hart stuck to her word. Her daughter remembered how 'she would change her clothes from whatever she'd been wearing for dinner in the evening and get into a long woollen dress and her shoes and everything, and sit down in the cabin to read, sew, or knit, and remain wide awake the whole night.' The daughter also admitted that she began to feel apprehensive because she sensed her mother's fear.

During the night of April 13-14, Mrs. Hart heard an odd sound and sent her husband on deck to see what was wrong. He came back and said it was just the sound of small pieces of ice hitting the side of the ship.

The next day was Sunday, and Mrs. Hart attended the church service. She then went to dinner, where one of the ship's officers, who was aware of her belief that the ship faced danger, asked her if she had 'given up taking care of the ship.' She replied that her vigil would continue.

It was 11.40pm when Mrs. Hart felt a jolt 'like a train pulling into the station.' She woke her husband, and reluctantly he agreed to go on deck to see what had happened. Upon his return, Eva noticed the worried look on her father's face. Telling his wife, 'You

RMS Titanic in Cork harbour, April 11, 1912.

better put this thick coat on', they then made their way to the deck. Mrs. Hart and her daughter were placed into a lifeboat and watched as Mr. Hart was lost to view as the boat was lowered into the water. They never saw him again.

In later years, Eva Hart reflected, 'If my mother hadn't been sitting up that night, I wouldn't be here now. I owe my life to her premonition. Don't I?'

JUMPING SHIP

One survivor, Elizabeth Dowdell, was quoted in the April 20, 1912, issue of the *Hudson Dispatch* as saying, 'We thought it a joke at the time when arriving at Queenstown to have heard three sailors remark that they would not continue their contemplated voyage on board the *Titanic*, for they had a dreadful fear of some disaster. They got off the ship and bade us farewell.'

She also confirmed to the newspaper that a large number of passengers she had encountered during the voyage also had a sense of impending disaster.

THE VISION

George Prangnell had been working for the White Star Line since 1909. On April 10, he said farewell to his wife Louisa and their sons and joined the *Titanic* to work in the engine room.

Mrs. Prangnell learned of the disaster and soon found herself waiting at the White Star offices in Southampton for news. Her children were left in the charge of an elderly babysitter who suddenly saw George Prangnell in a vision while staring into the flames of the fireplace. He appeared to be floating in the sea and was clinging to a life raft. The wife was told, and it was hoped, that this vision was a genuine sign that her husband was safe.

A cable eventually arrived, informing Mrs. Prangnell that her husband was indeed alive. As the ship sank, he jumped into the sea and swam to the side of a life raft. He then fastened his braces around the craft to stay afloat until he could be picked up by one of the lifeboats.

A SENSE OF DANGER

Mr. L. Gatti had been the restaurant manager of the *Olympic* but had been transferred to the *Titanic* for her maiden voyage. He left a wife behind at Southampton.

It was the night of April 14, and Mrs. Gatti was at home when, for no apparent reason, she began to feel a sense of danger. This feeling continued the next day and became so bad that she decided to visit her sister, where she learned of the *Titanic* disaster. Her husband never returned to her.

A WARNING IGNORED AND A LIFE SAVED

In 1912, my grandmother was 12 years old. She came from a poor family and had little hope of a bright future in the poverty-stricken area of London where the family lived. She was naturally excited to learn that an aunt had offered to take her on the *Titanic* with her own two children to start a new life in America. As you can imagine, she was terribly upset and disappointed to learn that her mother had refused to let her go.

Her mother told the aunt 'that something awful would happen' if she sailed on the Titanic. The aunt laughed off her warning and booked a place for herself and her children in the steerage section of the liner. All three went down with the ship. Their bodies were never found.

ANOTHER WARNING IS IGNORED

In 1912, Mary Richardson of Boaler Street in Liverpool had three dreams in succession of a ship sinking. She was later reading about the Titanic in a newspaper and realised that the ship was identical to the one in her dreams. Mrs. Richardson then learned that a cousin, Richard Fenton Butler, a mechanical engineer from Southsea, had booked a place on the liner. She wrote to him and asked if he would cancel his ticket. He refused and went down with the ship.

THE SHIP IS GOING TO ROLL OVER

Mr. W. Ward had been shipwrecked five times during his career as a steward on American liners. He had moved to Southampton with his wife and son, Jackie, after joining the

White Star Line. His first job with them was on the *Titanic*. His young son, after learning this, asked him not to sail with her as 'the ship was going to roll over.' This warning went unheeded, and he joined the *Titanic* as planned.

When his wife learned that the ship had sunk, she joined the other wives of crew members at the company offices to learn if her husband had survived. Two days went by without any news, and she naturally feared the worst. However, her son was sure that his father had survived, as he had dreamed three times in succession that his father, mother, and himself had all gone to the 'pictures' together. His conviction that the family would be together again proved true when, on April 19, a cable arrived from his father confirming that he had survived. Touchingly, the young boy was so happy at this news that he ran into a local newspaper office with the cable, shouting that his dad had been saved.

Chapter Six

THE TITANIC AND W.T. STEAD

William Thomas Stead was one of the most famous figures of the late 19th century. Stead was a journalist and a social reformer, and he was recognised as one of the leading figures of Spiritualism in Victorian and Edwardian Britain.

In 1912, Stead was due to attend a peace conference in America and had booked passage on the *Titanic*. History records that after the liner struck the iceberg, Stead helped several women and children into the lifeboats, even giving his life jacket to a fellow passenger. Several passengers recalled seeing Stead calmly reading a book in the smoking room as the ship started to sink. His body was never found.

It soon emerged that Stead had received several messages concerning the impending disaster but had ignored them all. These included direct warnings from psychics and even apparent precognitive predictions from his own hand.

So why had Stead, a committed believer in Spiritualism, turned a deaf ear to the mounting psychic evidence that something terrible was going to happen to him? Was it simply a case of hubris or just a perverse desire to challenge fate?

Read on and decide for yourself.

SUBCONSCIOUS PRECOGNITION?

In 1886, Stead wrote a story for the *Pall Mall Gazette* titled 'How a Mail Steamer went down in the mid-Atlantic.' This told of the sinking of a liner and the loss of a large number of its passengers due to a lack of lifeboats. Concluding the story, he said, 'This is exactly what might take place and what will take place if the liners are sent to sea short of boats.'

In December 1892, Stead wrote a story called *From the Old World to the New*. This concerned the loss of a ship after hitting an iceberg in the North Atlantic. Survivors of the disaster were rescued by the *Majestic*. Three years later, the real-life *Majestic* was captained by E.J. Smith. Smith was later named captain of the *Titanic*.

In 1909, Stead was speaking at the Cosmos Club in London. He was unhappy with the Society of Psychical Research, as he believed that they were being too scientific in their research and conclusions when it came to the idea of communication with the spirit

W.T. Stead.

world. During his speech, he used the image of himself drowning at sea and said, 'Suppose that instead of throwing me a rope, the rescuers should shout back, "Who are you? What is your name?" "I am Stead, W.T. Stead! I am drowning here in the sea! Throw me the rope. Be quick!"'

Stead then spoke of the rescuers ignoring his pleas and requesting information about his birth and the name of his grandmother to confirm that it was really him.

Stead concluded, 'Well, that is pretty typical of the "help" given by the S.P.R. to the friends who are trying to make us hear them from the Other Side!'

TERESINA

In January 1892, *Pearson's Magazine* published an article on palmistry in which 'Teresina' looked at the palm prints of nine individuals. The palmist was not told their names. Stead was one of the nine. 'Teresina' predicted that Stead would die when he was 63. Stead was unimpressed, as another psychic, Madame Blavatsky, had already told him he would live beyond 75. Stead was just short of his 63rd birthday when he boarded the Titanic.

MADAME DE THEBES

Madame de Thebes, a psychic, warned Stead in 1906 that he faced danger by water. 'Stead laughed at me then and said that he would have due warning from his familiars in the spirit world if any danger menaced him. Since that time, he had joked with me on more than one occasion about my premonition, pointing to his various long journeys accomplished without mishap. I only repeated my warning.'

STEAD'S VISION AND FOREBODING

Stead often spoke of his death and told friends of 'a vision of a mob, and this had made me feel that I shall not die in a way common to the most of us, but by violence, and one of many in a throng'.

In 1907, during a visit to Toronto, Stead again referred to this vision, saying he would either be kicked to death by a London mob or die in a disaster involving hundreds of others.

Before sailing on the *Titanic*, Stead's secretary, Edith Harper, recalled that he appeared very sombre, unlike his previous trips abroad. He confided in her, 'Something was going to happen somewhere, or somehow. And that it will be for good.'

ETTA WRIEDT

In May 1911, Stead was at a private séance with Etta Wriedt, an American who was considered an outstanding direct-voice medium. A spirit claiming to be a Native American warned Stead of impending death: 'Chief Steady! You cross big pond one time more, before you shuttee eye!'

Etta Wriedt.

MORE WARNINGS

In September 1911, Stead had a reading with W. de Kerlor, a palm reader and psychic. Upon looking at Stead's palm, he said, 'Your life will end tragically; it will end in public: you will either be trampled upon or kicked to death, in a most unexpected manner.'

Stead was not impressed but did agree to see de Kerlor again later that month, where the psychic again warned him of disaster: 'I see a triangular light above your head which looks very like the knife of a guillotine!' Stead laughed at this but allowed de Kerlor to continue with his reading.

De Kerlor then predicted that Stead's planned trip to Russia would not take place and he would travel to the US instead:, 'I can see nothing but the picture of a huge black ship, of which I see the back portion; where the name of the ship should be written, there is a wreath of immortelles … I can only see half the ship. That symbol may mean by the time this ship will be completed – when one will be able to see it in its whole length – it is perhaps then that you will go on your journey.'

De Kerlor later had a dream and contacted Stead to tell him about it: 'I dreamed I was in the midst of a catastrophe on the water. There were masses of bodies struggling in the water, and I was among them. I could hear the cries for help, and when the voices ceased, I could see some spirit forms climbing upwards, while others seemed to go downwards, and my soul was in the midst of them.'

De Kerlor also spoke of seeing over 1,000 bodies in the sea, but Stead was still untroubled by this latest vision.

In February 1912, de Kerlor was speaking to members of the International Psychic Club. By chance, Stead's private secretary, Edith Harper, was in attendance along with her mother, S.L. Adela Harper. De Kelor approached Miss Harper and asked her to pass on another warning to Stead.

Miss Harper later recalled how de Kerlor had 'described a huge ship, of which he could only see the back part. In place of the name of the ship, he saw a number of wreaths of immortelles. He took this to mean trouble and difficulty, and a very gloomy condition in connection with Mr. Stead. He also described another symbolic vision of a stone called an "agatha", in the midst of which Mr. Stead was standing with the veins of the stone encircling him. This denoted – Mr. de Kerlor said – limitations, difficulties, and troubles from which he could not free himself. The stone Mr. de Kerlor told me is symbolic of funerals and mourning and was described by the ancients to the malefic influence of the planet Saturn.'

Stead's last contact with the psychic was over the telephone. De Kerlor again repeated his warnings but was sharply rebuffed by the journalist, 'Oh yes; well, well, you are a very gloomy prophet. Goodbye.'

THE CRUCIFIX

In 1911, the apparent spirit of Catherine the Great appeared during a séance in England. A crucifix also appeared some 3in long. It was made of silver and ivory and featured a skull and crossbones at the base of the cross. On the reverse was a silver rose. It was supposedly once owned by the Russian empress.

Stead became the owner of the cross in December of the same year and showed it to his friends at a séance. One of the sitters, Mr. King, felt that the 'astral conditions' surrounding the cross were very bad and asked Stead to get rid of it. Stead declined. King then received messages from his spirit guides claiming that the cross was 'strongly charged with black magic' and had been used in a black mass. Stead was advised that contact with the crucifix would be harmful to all those not 'specially protected'.

Stead again declined to get rid of it, but within days he began to suffer from a bad bout of depression. Stead finally allowed a colleague, Mr. Skeels, to take the crucifix and have it 'demagnetized.' Following this, Stead's depression lifted, and he admitted that there 'might be something' in the curse after all. He added, however, that the whole idea of a cursed crucifix still sounded absurd.

The Titanic leaving Southampton on April 10, 1912.

Others who came into contact with the crucifix became ill, and Mr. King was still worried that the object held harmful energies and continued to warn Stead of his concerns.

On January 3, 1912, Stead found himself sharing lunch with Dr. Dillon of the *Daily Telegraph*. Stead told the journalist of the crucifix and the ill effects apparently associated with it: 'I have it now, and I am curious to see whether any mischief will befall me and what form it will take. Is it not thrilling?'

Stead even offered to lend the crucifix to Dillon to test 'its fatal potency,' but the newsman wisely declined.

It is not known if Stead took the crucifix with him when he boarded the *Titanic*. The crucifix was never seen again.

THE EGYPTIAN CURSE

It was the evening of April 12, and the *Titanic* was two days into her maiden voyage. Stead was in the first-class smoking room and was chatting with eight of his fellow passengers. The time was approaching midnight, and the subject turned to the supernatural. Stead decided to tell those gathered a story that he claimed had never been told by him before:, 'To prove I am not superstitious, I call your attention to the fact that it was Friday when I began this story, and the day of its ending, my watch tells me, will fall upon a 13th.'

Stead then told of an Egyptian mummy case and an inscription on it that warned that anyone who repeated verbally the story told on it would meet with a violent death. Stead then repeated the tale on the case.

The last known photograph of the Titanic. It was taken at Crosshaven, Co Cork, Ireland, just after the ship departed Queenstown.

The only known picture of Titanic's wireless radio room.

Fred Seward was the only one of the eight men to survive the sinking. He told reporters when asked about the cursed story on the mummy case, 'I guess, on the whole, it is not a story that I will ever tell.'

SÉANCES

After Stead's death, numerous mediums claimed to have been in contact with him. Many of the messages given were very general and offered little to convince the sceptic that Stead had really communicated through them.

However, there were other séances where Stead was both seen and heard by people who had known him in life. The sceptics will find these accounts harder to dismiss.

Etta Wriedt was to have accompanied Stead to England on his return trip on the *Titanic* so that her psychic gifts could be studied and observed in London.

Stead's spirit first appeared to the medium on April 17 in New York. Vice Admiral William Usborne Moore, a retired British naval commander turned psychical researcher, was present and described what happened: 'He was weak in articulation, but we quite understood him. His stay was short. The next night, Thursday, Mr. Stead came again; his articulation and personality were much stronger, and he went into details of his passing. The following night, Friday, he came again very strong and clear, again giving us full details of his passing. He particularly desired that Mrs. Wriedt go over to London to fulfil her engagement, which she is now about doing.'

The sinking of the Titanic based on a description by Jack Thayer, a first class passenger. He was one of only a handful of passengers to survive jumping into the icy sea.

The sinking of the Titanic by Willy Stöwer.

The Titanic leaves Cork Harbour for New York.

Mrs. Wriedt travelled to England and, on May 5, held a séance in Wimbledon. Moore was also there, and they both saw and conversed with Stead. He 'gave three admirable tests of his identity', which included details about a conversation held between Stead and Moore the last time they had met.

The following day, Estelle Stead, Stead's daughter, took part in a sitting with the medium. 'Three weeks after the *Titanic* disaster, I saw my father's head and shoulders, as plainly as I saw them when we last met on Earth. I talked to him about the most intimate things concerning myself and him alone – things about which the medium could have no possible idea. It was a trumpet séance … After showing his face, my father took the trumpet and, turning to one of the sitters, who had been somewhat sceptical at our previous sittings, when father was present in his psychical body, said most emphatically, "Do you believe now? Is not all I told you true?"

Admiral Moore, who was also present, wrote, 'At least 40 minutes were taken up by Stead talking to his daughter. I could not help hearing every word. It was the most painful and, at the same time, the most realistic, convincing conversation I have ever heard in my investigations.'

Ten days later, another séance was held with Mrs. Wriedt. Stead appeared this time to his friend, Count Chedo Miyatovich: 'There in that slowly moving light was, not the spirit, but the very person of my friend William T. Stead, not wrapped in white, but in his usual walking costume.'

Stead then conversed with Miyatovich: 'Yes, I am Stead. William T. Stead. My dear friend, Miyatovich, I came here expressly to give you fresh proof that there is life after death. You always hesitated to accept that truth.'

Miyatovich replied that he had believed what Stead had told him. Stead replied, 'You believed because I was telling you something about it; now I come here to bring you proof that you should not only believe but know that there really is a life after death.' Stead then introduced a female friend of Miyatovich who had died just three weeks before.

A supper was held on May 29 at William Stead's home in Wimbledon. Mrs. Wriedt was in attendance along with Estelle Stead and several members of Julia's Bureau, a group of psychics originally brought together by her father to communicate with the Other Side. The name Julia was taken from a deceased friend of Stead's called Julia Ames, who had been acting as his spirit guide.

William Stead's chair was placed at the head of the table and was occupied by a potted bush. Felicia Scatcherd noticed that another of the guests, Mr. Mallinson, was looking at the plant. 'I followed Mr. Mallinson's gaze to the blossoms nearest to Mrs. Wriedt,' recalled Felicia. 'They were in an agitated movement, one after the other, then all together. The rest of the plant was quiet. But as I looked, the topmost blossom moved alone; later, others "bowed".

'"Now move the whole plant!" I exclaimed. It turned, pot and all, towards me.'

Miss Scratcherd then asked for the chair to move. The chair turned and moved towards her by several inches. The walls, floor and windows also started to vibrate, shattering

The Titanic's Collapsible Boat D is photographed from RMS Carpathia on April 15, 1912.

Titanic's wooden lifeboats in New York Harbour following the disaster.

crockery in the process. One of the sitters, Mrs. Harper, the mother of Stead's secretary, called out, 'That's right, chief! Keep your word!' and three violent shocks rattled the windows. Loud footsteps were also heard, as if someone were stomping around the room.

Some of those present asked Mrs. Harper what she meant by crying out, 'That's right, chief! Keep your word!' She explained that Stead, two weeks before leaving on the *Titanic*, had attended a séance where only very faint rapping had been heard.

'When I come back,' he said, 'I shall stamp around the room and shake the floors, and windows. There will be no mistake me being there!' Others confirmed that Stead had said this.

Another séance with Mrs. Wriedt was held on June 18, 1912. In attendance was W. de Kerlor – the man who had tried to warn Stead of impending doom – along with others, including Edith Harper and W.B. Yates, the Irish poet and playwright. De Kelor saw Stead appear before him. The figure then spoke, 'My dear Mr. de Kelor – my dear boy - forgive me for not having taken heed of the predictions and warnings you gave me.'

Stead went on to explain to the other sitters how he had ignored de Kerlor's warnings and then said how he had died. Stead claimed that a blow to the head had killed him after falling from the liner as the stern rose out of the water during her last minutes of life.

De Kerlor wrote, 'The manifestation was so real, the voice so exactly like his when alive, the words and emphatic assertions in every detail so like himself – so complete, so impressive, and the reality of Mr. Stead's personality so tangible, that when the voice ceased, one almost asked oneself whether he had not been bodily present. It seemed incredible that we had been listening to one who had so recently passed to the great beyond.'

De Kerlor attended another séance with Mrs. Wriedt on June 25. Stead again came through, and de Kerlor asked if Stead could assist him in a lecture to the International Psychic Club to be held the following day. Stead replied that it clashed with his own memorial service, something he wished to attend, but would nevertheless do his best to help. He then expressed happiness that Dr. Wallace would be chairing the meeting at the club.

De Kerlor was surprised at this statement, as Wallace had not confirmed his attendance and no one but de Kerlor was even aware that he had been asked to chair the meeting. It was only on the day of the meeting that Wallace called the psychic to confirm he would be there!

So did Stead return from the dead and speak with the living? The sceptic will claim that his appearances were based on trickery and the gullibility of the sitters. But what of the fact that several people who all knew Stead personally, including his daughter, all recognised the journalist's face and voice? Were they all mistaken? And what of the personal information known only to Stead and his daughter, or Stead's foreknowledge that Dr. Wallace would be chairing the meeting that de Kerlor was about to attend, something unknown to the other sitters or the medium? How can all these facts be explained away as fraud or wishful thinking?

Sir Arthur Conan Doyle once said that he regarded Mrs. Wriedt as the best direct-voice medium in the world. The evidence, as witnessed by Stead's daughter, Miyatovich, de Kerlor, and others, would suggest that he was right.

I will end this chapter by quoting William Stead himself. The message was recorded using automatic writing and was relayed to Stead's daughter by another medium, Pardoe Woodman: 'Life here is a grander thing - a bolder thing - and a happier thing for all those who have led reasonable lives on earth, but for the unreasonable, there are many troubles and difficulties, and sorrows to be encountered. There is a great truth in the saying that "as ye sow, so shall ye reap".'

Chapter Seven

THE WEEPING LADY OF
HOLY TRINITY CHURCH,
MICKLEGATE, YORK

For over 300 years, it was said that ghosts haunted the grounds of Holy Trinity, especially the area below the eastern side of the church. The ghosts were often seen during morning services and were only visible to the congregation in the upstairs gallery, who were able to witness the figures through the east window. The story became widely known after the Rev. Sabine Baring-Gould, author of *Onward, Christian Soldiers*, wrote about the case in *Yorkshire Oddities*, a book first published in the 1870s.

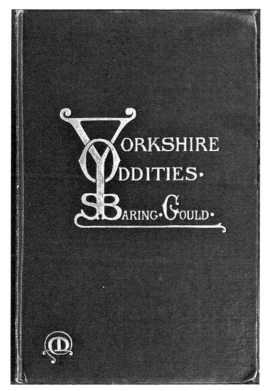

The author's interest in the haunting was piqued after an old acquaintance, a clergyman, wrote to him in 1869 with the suggestion that he may wish to look into the puzzling events connected with the medieval church of Holy Trinity in York. Strange figures had been seen by the clergyman, and he was at a loss to explain the reason behind their appearance.

Sabine Baring-Gould first wrote about the haunting of Holy Trinity Church in his book, Yorkshire Oddities.

75

Sabine Baring-Gould.

The clergyman's own account of the haunting was dated 1866 and read as follows: 'While staying in York at this time last year (1865), or perhaps a little earlier, I first heard of the apparitions or ghosts supposed to be seen in Trinity Church, Micklegate. I felt curious

The East Window today.

to see a ghost, I confess, if such a thing is to be seen without the usual concomitants of a dark night and a lone house. Accordingly, I went to the church for morning service on a blazing hot Sunday morning in August last with a girl about 13 years old and her little brother.

'The east window of the church, I must explain, is of stained glass, rather tawdry and of no particular design, except that the colouring is much richer in the centre than at the sides, and that at the extreme edge, there is one pane of unstained glass which runs all round the window.

'The peculiarity of the apparition is that it is seen on the window itself, rather less than halfway from the bottom (as I saw it from the gallery), and has much the same effect as that of a slide drawn through a magic lantern when seen on the exhibiting sheet. The form seen – I am told invariably – is that of a figure dressed in white walking across the window, and gives the idea of someone passing in the churchyard in a surplice. I say a figure, for the number is generally limited to one, and I was told that only on Trinity Sunday did more than one appear, and that then there were three.

'But I can vouch for the larger number appearing on other occasions, as on the day I was there, which was one of the Sundays after Trinity, there were rarely fewer than three visible.

'The figures began to move across the window long before the commencement of the service, when in fact there was no one present but ourselves. They did so again before the service began, as well as during the "Venite", and subsequently as many as 20 or 30 times, I should suppose, till the conclusion of the sermon.

'Of the three figures, two were evidently those of women, and the third was a little child. The two women were very distinct in appearance. One was tall and very graceful, and the other middle-sized; we called the second one the nursemaid, from her evident care of the child during the absence of the mother, which relationship we attributed to the tall one, from the passionate affection she exhibited towards the child, her caressing it, and the wringing of her hands over it.

'I may add that each figure is perfectly distinct from the others, and after they had been seen once or twice, are at once recognisable.

'The order of their proceedings, with slight variation, was this: The mother came alone from the north side of the window, and having gone about halfway across, stopped, turned round, and waved her arm towards the quarter whence she had come. This signal was answered by the entry of the nurse with the child. Both figures then bent over the child and seemed to bemoan its fate, but the taller one was always the most endearing in her gestures. The mother then moved towards the other side of the window, taking the child with her, leaving the nurse in the centre of the window, from which she gradually retired towards the north corner, whence she had come, waving her hand, as though making signs of farewell, as she retreated.

'After some little time, she again appeared, bending forward and evidently anticipating the return of the other two, who never failed to reappear from the south side of the window where they had disappeared.

'The same gestures of despair and distress were repeated, and then all three retired together to the north side of the window.

'Usually, they appeared during the musical portions of the service, and especially during one long eight-line hymn, when – for the only occasion without the child – the two women rushed on (in stage phrase) and remained during the whole hymn, making the most frantic gestures of despair. Indeed, the louder the music in that hymn, the more carried away with their grief did they seem to be.

'Nothing could be more emphatic than the individuality of the several figures; the manner of each had its own peculiarity. I do not doubt that if the stained glass were removed, a much plainer view would be obtained. I think so because the nearer the centre of the window, where the stained glass was thickest, there the less distinct were the forms. It was like catching glimpses of them through leaves. But nearer the edge of the window, where the colours were less bright, they were perfectly distinct, and still more so on the pane of unstained glass at the edge. There they seemed most clear and gave one the impression of being real persons, not shadows.

'Indeed, by far the most remarkable and perplexing incident in the whole spectacle was this, that on one occasion, when the mother and child had taken their departure, the medium figure – the nurse – waved her hands, and after walking slowly to the very edge of the window, turned round whilst on the pane of unstained glass, and waved her arm towards the other two with what one would call a stage gesture, and then I most distinctly saw, and I emphatically declare I did see the arm bare nearly to the shoulder, with beautiful folds of white drapery hanging from it like a picture on a Greek vase.

'Nothing could be plainer than the drag of the robes on the ground after the figures as they retired at the edge of the window where the clear glass was, previous to going out. The impression produced was that one saw real persons in the churchyard; for though the figures were seen on the window, yet they gave one the impression of walking past the window outside and not moving upon the glass.

'No one in the church seemed to be in the smallest degree attracted or discomposed by all this or, indeed, to observe it.

'I talked a great deal on the subject with Miss C——, daughter of the late Dr C—— of York, and she told me that Mr W——, the Incumbent of Trinity Church, would give anything to get rid of it or discover the imposture if imposture there be. She told me that he and his family had watched day and night without being able to find any clue to the mystery. Their house is in the churchyard and opposite the east window, and therefore very favourably placed for such an investigation. I am not inclined to think that the trees outside the church at the east end can originate the appearance by any optical illusions produced by waving branches. I could see their leaves rustling in the air, and their movement was evidently unconnected with the appearance and movement of the figures.'

Baring-Gould was greatly intrigued by this account and decided to make further inquiries into the haunting. He soon received several other letters that echoed what the clergyman had seen.

Here is one example:

York, 28 March 1874

Sir,

Owing to severe illness in my family, I was not able to reply to your note earlier. I will now try and tell you what I have seen and been told on the subject of the ghosts at Holy Trinity Church, Micklegate.

A York lady, now dead, told me she remembered seeing it when a child and that she once read an account of it in an old History of York; she thought the book must have been published in the 17th century.

We now live in the parish of Holy Trinity and attend the church regularly. A part of my family sit in the gallery; therefore, I will tell you, in as matter-of-fact a manner as possible, what I myself have seen, and leave one of my daughters, if she likes, to give you her experiences.

I must state also that the ghost is seen more or less distinctly as you happen to be seated in the centre or side of the gallery; as a rule, the former is the best place.

As I have no faith in ghosts, I have been most wishful to have the matter cleared up. At present, I cannot account for the appearance in any way.

I went many times to the gallery in hopes of seeing the phenomenon but was repeatedly disappointed. At last, one dull day, hopeless for the purpose as I thought – rain was falling at the time – I was startled by seeing something.

There are two east windows – one on the right, filled with common green glass, the organ in front of it. From the outside of this window, I saw something move, and immediately a graceful figure of a girl of 18 or 20 years crossed the outside of the stained east window with a light, free step. She was entirely covered with a fine lace veil, which, as she walked and met the air, showed the outline of the head and figure; the features I could not distinguish, but could see a shade through the veil where they naturally would be.

The veil was of a pure white, flowing back as a train as she walked. In two or three minutes, the figure returned, the robe flowing back in the same way, and disappeared behind the organ window.

The figure appeared to me to be decidedly outside the window, and at a greater distance than was possible for anyone to be; in the first place, because the east window is high up, and therefore anyone walking past it, to be seen at all, must be at some little distance from it; and, secondly, because there is a dead wall within a few yards of the window.

The pure white of the robe quite obliterated the colours in the window, but the lead work was distinct enough, and the figure appeared behind it. The distinct outline of the figure is most striking.

The apparition always returns to the organ window. I have seen this several times since the first. Owing to the dull day and the darkness of the windows, the appearance on the first occasion was the more remarkable. Two or three other figures also appear, but I never thought them as distinct as the first, and I thought the second and third might be reflections of the first. The two or three often move quickly back and forwards with a dancing movement somewhat like the reflection of the sun on a wall, but taking the form of human figures. However, it was dull and raining when first I saw the apparition, so that on that occasion there could have been no reflection of sunlight.

These appearances are sometimes not seen for weeks and months, then they appear once or twice on succeeding days or Sundays. No one can be sure of seeing them if they go to the church for that purpose. I do not believe the apparition takes place at one more favoured time than another, though some people like to think so. The present rector wished to abolish the 'ghosts,' and was advised to cut down one or two trees. This was done, all thought that the ghosts were banished. Ten months after there was a gay wedding my daughters went into the gallery to witness the ceremony, and lo! the 'ghost or ghosts' were there also. They had not been seen for nine or ten months. That was the first occasion since the cutting down of the trees on which they reappeared.

The Sunday-school children who sit in the gallery see the form so often as to be quite familiar with the sight and call them 'the mother, nurse, and child.'

The legend I have heard told of it is that a family, consisting of a father, mother, and only child, lived here once upon a time. The father died and was buried at the east end of the church, under or near the organ window. After a while, the plague broke out in York and carried off the child, and it was buried outside the city, as those who died of plague were not allowed to be laid in the churchyards for fear of communicating the infection.

The mother died afterwards and was laid in her husband's grave, and now, as in her lifetime, continues to visit the grave of her child and bemoan the separation. The child is brought from its grave in the plague-pit by the mother and nurse and brought to the grave of its father, and then it is taken back to where it lies outside the walls.

L.S.

Another letter to Baring-Gould read as follows:

South Parade, York

March 22, 1871

Dear Mr. Baring-Gould,

I promised to send you an account of the ghost at Holy Trinity, Micklegate, and I now forward you the enclosed, written by a friend on whose word you may perfectly rely.

I heard another account a few days ago from a lady who saw it on Sunday, the 19th February last. She described the figure – for she saw only one – as being dressed in a shining white garment, and says that it crossed the east window twice, with a slightly 'skipping' step. It appeared to be outside the church, as she saw it distinctly through the stained glass.

I have never seen it myself, though I have been several times to the church.

There are four lights in the east window, and the glass of the two central lights is of a darker tint than that in the side ones. There are, however, narrow panes of transparent glass in each of the lights, so that a person passing across the window outside could be distinctly seen by anyone sitting in the west gallery.

The sill of the east window is about five feet from the ground outside and about seven feet from the pavement inside; about ten yards from the east wall separating the churchyard from a private garden.

Yours very truly,

R.T.

This is the enclosure alluded to by R.T. 'Having heard from several people of the ghost at the Church of the Holy Trinity, Micklegate, York, on Sunday, at the end of September 1869, a friend and myself made up our minds to go and see if we, also could be favoured with a sight of this wonderful apparition.

'Well, we went up into the gallery, the only place whence they say it is to be seen. You may, perhaps, already know that the gallery faces the east window, which is filled with modern stained glass.

Holy Trinity Church.

'I am afraid that our attention rambled somewhat from the service, for we were looking out for the ghostly visitant. However, we watched and watched, as we began to think, in vain, until at the very end of the second lesson, when, just before the beginning of the "Jubilate Deo", I saw a figure, I should say of a shortish woman, with something white folded over her, covering even her head and face, but still I could see what it was. The figure appeared to walk very fast across the two middle lights of the east window, from right to left (i.e., from south to north), and seemed to be at some distance from the window.

'The strange thing is that I saw it clearly through the thick painted glass.

'The whole thing happened so suddenly and really surprised me so much, that for some time I could hardly get up from the seat or find my place at the beginning of the chant. Just as it disappeared, my friend said, "Did you see that?" To which, of course, I answered, "Yes; did you?" That was all we saw, and a lady who was there at the same time, whom we knew, saw it also, exactly as we did, only apparently not with the same distinctness.

'Many persons have seen a great deal more. I believe that the figure is generally seen to walk across the window in the reverse way to that which my friend and I saw and returns with a child, some say with two.

'We examined outside the window. It is a good deal above the ground, about five feet, I should think, and at the side of it is a very old gravestone with no inscription on the headstone as far as I could make out. I believe it is currently reported that the apparition issues from that grave.

'Some people thought that it might be a shadow caused in some peculiar manner by the trees that grew outside; but it was not, for the trees were cut down about three years ago, and the apparition is still seen, as it has been, I have been told, for a century.

'I have nothing to add, except that this is a true and unexaggerated account of what I saw.'

Letters about the haunting started to appear in the press. Here is one example from the *Newcastle Daily Chronicle,* dated 1874:

Sir,

On Good Friday last, I went to Holy Trinity Church, York, for morning service at 11 o'clock and repaired with a friend to the gallery, being anxious to see a certain apparition which is said to haunt the place.

The gallery is situated at the extreme west end of the building and faces the east window, from which it is distant some 50 feet or so. It is said that in the aisle and body of the church, nothing is ever seen. The gallery was full, but no one seemed to have come there, especially for the ghost, and though many of them afterwards said they saw it, they were not in the least affected by the apparition, treating it as a matter of course, to which they were well accustomed.

I kept my eyes fixed upon the east window for nearly the whole of the hour and a half during which the service lasted, but was not favoured with a sight of the phenomenon; although others saw it cross the window and return, and my friend, who knows it well, called my attention to the fact at the moment, yet I could not perceive nothing. I, therefore, left the place as unbelieving as ever and supposed that either I was the victim of a hoax or that it required a great stretch of imagination to fancy that a passing shadow was the desired object. However, not liking to discredit the statements of many friends who were used to seeing it almost every Sunday, I consented on Easter Day to go to the same place and pew. The seat I occupied was not an advantageous one, a large brass chandelier being between me and the lower panes of the window.

In the middle of the service, my eyes, which had hardly once moved from the left or north side of the window, were attracted by a bright light formed like a female robed and hooded passing from north to south with a rapid gliding motion outside the church apparently at some distance. The window is Gothic and I fancy from 20 to 25 feet high by 12 to 15 feet wide at the base. The panes through which the ghost shines are about 5 feet high and about halfway between the top and bottom.

There are four divisions in the window, all of stained glass, of no particular pattern, the outer on right and left being of lighter colour than the two centre panes, and at the edge of each runs a rim of plain transparent white glass, about two inches wide, and adjoining the stonework. Through this rim, especially, could be seen what looked like a form transparent but yet thick (if such a term can be used) with light. It did not resemble linen, for instance, but was far brighter and would, no doubt, have been dazzling to a near observer. The robe was long and trailed. The figure was, of course, not visible when it had crossed the window and passed behind the wall.

My friend whispered to me that it would return, must return, and at the end of five minutes or so, the same figure glided back from right to left, having turned round while out of sight. About half an hour later it again passed across from north to south, and having remained about ten seconds only, returned with what I believe to have been the figure of a young child and stopped at the last pane but one, where both vanished. I did not see the child again, but a few seconds afterwards the woman reappeared and completed the passage, behind the last pane, very rapidly. Nothing more was seen during the service, and no other opportunity presented itself to me for making observations. During each time, the chandelier prevented me from obtaining a complete view, but there could be no doubt as to the shape, a certain amount of indistinctness, however, being caused by the stained glass.

On the reappearance for the last time, I saw the head, which was, I believe, that of the child, move up and down distinctly as if nodding. The figure shone with dazzling brightness and appeared to be at a considerable distance, say 30 yards or so, though at the same time as distinct as possible, considering the obstruction of coloured glass.

Each time the level upon which it glided was precisely the same, and afterwards, on carrying a straight line from the spot in the gallery where I sat, through the part of the glass where the feet of the figure shone, and continuing that line (in my mind's eye, with all the objects before me, except the ghost, whose position I had taken good notice of), I found that it would traverse a thick holly tree eight or nine feet high at about four feet from the ground, and at two or three feet from the ground a low wall about four feet high, and would reach the ground itself in the middle of a gravel yard belonging to the back premises of the house, called the vicarage, at a distance of 12 or 15 yards from the window. Any person walking between the window and the holly tree would barely be seen at all, much less be seen in the place which the apparition occupies, and any one on the further side of the tree would be almost, if not quite invisible on account of the holly and other bushes and the dead wall. Anyone about there at all can easily be seen from the many houses on all sides.

If it were a shadow thrown upon the glass of the window, it would, of course, be seen by those who sit in the body of the church as well as those in the gallery.

It cannot be a reflection on the principle of Pepper's Ghost, which is produced by the figure actually being in a very strong light and appearing reflected on glass in a darkish spot. The lights both inside and outside of the church at York, which might be thought to produce the ghost, are precisely the reverse, and any figure required to be reproduced by reflection on the east window would have to be standing or walking in the centre of the aisle.

For the above facts, I can vouch, and I have no reason to believe that the following are either incorrect or exaggerated.

It is said (the ghost) to appear very frequently on Trinity Sunday and to bring two other figures onto the scene, another female called the nurse and the child. It is often seen as distinctly on a dark, rainy, or snowy day as when the sun is shining. When I saw it, the sun was not bright.

The motion is even, not at all jerky. Sometimes it glides swiftly, at other times slowly. It cannot be a mere accidental reflection, from a door or window, for instance, for the figure faces different ways according to the direction in which it is going, and it is not always alone, nor do the figures always act in concert.

One of my friends, with a companion, has watched outside on the wall, where he had a full view of the whole place around, during morning service. The ghost has been seen from the inside, while outside nothing was visible.

It is said to have haunted the church for 150, 200, and some authorities say 300 years, and there are many pretty legends connected with it.

One of the many traditions says that 300 years ago, during religious disturbances, a party of soldiers came to sack the convent attached to this church; that the abbess, a woman of great virtue and courage, stopped them as they were entering, declaring that they should enter over her dead body only, and that, should they succeed in their sacrilegious purpose, as they afterwards did, her spirit would haunt the place until the true Church was re-established and a convent built on the same spot. Another story relates that during the plague some 200 years ago, a nurse and child died of the pestilence and were necessarily buried outside the city walls, while the unfortunate mother of the child, at her death, was interred in Holy Trinity Churchyard. Here the mother waits and receives the nurse and child, weeping and wringing her hands before parting with them. The same scene is often enacted several times during the same day and even during the same service.

Whatever may have been the circumstances under which the ghost (if it is one, which it is hard to believe in these matter-of-fact days) commenced its peculiar promenade, I would recommend those who have the chance to go to Holy Trinity Church, York, and see for themselves, though an audience of the apparition cannot always be assured. A ghost in broad daylight does no harm, frightens no one, and ought to interest everybody.

I am, etc.

H.G.F.T.

What is striking to any observer is that several independent witnesses all saw the same thing. Another strange feature of the case was that the figures were sometimes described as appearing both 'on' and 'beyond' the stained glass of the window.

As you can imagine, the church authorities were less than pleased with all this publicity. The rector of Holy Trinity wrote an angry letter to the *York Herald*, stating that the ghosts were 'fabricated by a morbid imagination.' He claimed that the apparitions were people, very much alive, walking about in the vicarage garden behind the church. He also warned sensation seekers to stay away, as the church was 'God's house, intended to be a house of prayer and not a place for gratifying an idle curiosity.'

Others quickly wrote in support of the rector. It was claimed that the ghosts were caused either by the sun's reflection from another building or by trees swaying in the wind.

All these explanations soon collapsed upon further inspection. The ghosts were often seen on gloomy days, so a reflection from a nearby building could easily be ruled out. The trees in the churchyard had been cut down three years before and could not be blamed for causing the figures to appear. And let us not forget the letter in the *Newcastle Daily Chronicle*, where the author clearly stated that a man had been stationed outside the church in order to observe the churchyard during the service. He had seen nothing, and yet the figures had once again been seen through the east window by those sitting inside.

The strange apparitions continued to be seen until the 1880s, when major alterations were made to the church. The east window and gallery were replaced – some said as a direct result of the haunting – and after that, the figures were never again seen from inside the church. One theory suggests that certain ghosts are caused by the release of intense emotions. This energy is then recorded by the stones or bricks of a building. The images are then replayed under certain atmospheric or environmental conditions. A sensitive

The interior of Holy Trinity (Figgis-West).

person, such as a medium, may also be able to tune into them. Alterations to a structure may cause the phenomenon to be erased for good or, in some cases, even lead to an increase in activity.

As stated earlier in this chapter, a local tradition maintained that the ghost was that of a prioress who was murdered when Henry VIII's soldiers came to shut down a convent that stood on the site. However, this story can safely be dismissed as the last prioress, Isobel Warde, was allowed to retire and live out the rest of her life in another part of the city. Another legend claimed that the figures were those of a mother, a nurse, and her child, the child having died of the plague. Did the mental anguish of a grieving mother praying in the church centuries ago cause the image of herself, her nurse, and her beloved child to be projected into the very fabric of Holy Trinity? Or was this additional story simply created in order to provide a convenient explanation for the haunting?

And what of Holy Trinity in the decades following the publication of Baring-Gould's account of the haunting?

A woman in white was occasionally witnessed running through the churchyard in the immediate years following the Victorian alterations to the church. In 1957, a woman visiting the church noticed a change in the atmosphere near the spot where the gallery had once stood. She described it as being 'earthy and cold, a very charnel house atmosphere of death and decay.' She was not aware of the ghost stories connected with the church at the time of her visit.

It has now been over 140 years since Sabine Baring-Gould first made the world aware of the strange events in Holy Trinity, and yet the haunting still remains one of York's most puzzling mysteries and one that still defies explanation.

My recent inquiries into the haunting of Holy Trinity would seem to suggest that both the church and churchyard are now free from any paranormal activity. It appears that only tourists taking part in one of the city's many popular ghost walks and the incessant drone of nearby traffic now disturb what was once considered York's most haunted place.

Chapter Eight

THE GHOSTS OF DUNWICH

In 2018, I found myself on the Suffolk coast producing and acting in a film, *The Ghost of Winifred Meeks*, a ghost story written and directed by Jason Figgis.

It was partly filmed in a Victorian house in the village of Dunwich, a place which is no stranger to filmmaking as some of the scenes from Jonathan Miller's classic 1968 adaptation of an M.R. James story, *Oh, Whistle, and I'll Come to You, My Lad*, were filmed on the cliffs above the beach.

We even experienced some paranormal events during our stay in the Victorian house. Jason was in bed one night when he heard a woman shouting in the downstairs kitchen. At the time, all the cast and crew were safely asleep upstairs. Another night, I heard the sounds of a child crying from somewhere in the house. The next morning, Lara Belmont, our lead actress, found a child's handprint on the glass of her bedroom window. The imprint was on the outside of the glass, and her bedroom was one floor up with no means of access from the outside!

Julie Abbott as a troubled spirit in a scene from the film, The Ghost of Winifred Meeks (Jason Figgis).

It is hard to believe now, but Dunwich was once one of the most prosperous towns in all of England. It boasted nine churches, a palace, gilded gates, a circuit of defensive walls, a large harbour, and had a population of roughly 3,000 people.

Over the centuries, coastal erosion and terrible storms resulted in most of the town gradually being lost to the sea. Today, only a few streets and a scattering of buildings remain to remind us of its former glory.

During breaks between filming, I wandered around Dunwich and soon discovered from locals that the village was home to a large number of ghostly tales and legends.

There is a tradition that three crowns were buried in East Anglia during Saxon times to protect England from invasion. One was hidden in Dunwich but was lost when the town fell into the sea. Another was discovered in Rendlesham in the 18th century, but was sadly melted down for the gold. The third remains buried somewhere along the coast. M.R. James based his classic ghost story *A Warning to the Curious* on this legend. However, it should be noted that some scholars have suggested that the legend was invented by James himself, as there is no mention of it in any books on East Anglia before the publication of his story.

The 'Dark Heart of Dunwich' is a tale that dates back to the 12th century. Eva, a local girl, was due to be married to the son of a landowner but fell in love with another man, who promptly deserted her and fled to sea. She waited in vain for him to return and, in a final act of despair, cut out her heart and tossed it into the waves. Her ghost still haunts the beach, and the heart itself, now almost wooden-like in appearance, is believed to wash up on the shore from time to time. If you see it, do not be tempted to pick it up, as the object is cursed and will bring great misfortune to those who touch it!

It is said that you can still hear sunken church bells ringing out a mournful tune at night. Local fishermen believe that they are only heard before a storm. Divers often claim to experience an uneasy feeling and a sense of being watched when exploring the ruins beneath the waves. One said he felt someone standing on the seabed and watching him intently as he explored one of the submerged ruins.

The ghosts of the town's former inhabitants are said to haunt the shore below the cliffs. One of these, a man in Tudor clothing, has been seen walking towards the shoreline and stepping into a small boat, which then sails away. The ghostly laughter of children and the sounds of phantom cattle have also been heard along the sandy beach.

The Ship Inn has a ghost in the attic room. A former owner of the pub once claimed to have woken up in the night to discover a figure sitting at the end of her bed. It then got up and vanished through one of the walls. Building work several years later uncovered a hidden door at the very spot where the ghost disappeared.

The remains of the leper chapel, located next to St. James' Church, date from the 12th century. The area is home to several shapeless shadows that flit through the ruins. They are

The Ship Inn, Dunwich (John West).

believed to be the unhappy souls of those lepers who once worshipped there and now lie beneath the chapel floor.

The buttress of All Saint's Church stands nearby. Before 1918, a villager was told that a very old book contained a prediction that a ruined church tower on the cliffs would collapse at the end of the 'greatest war in history.' The tower of All Saints Church finally fell four years after the First World War ended.

A few years ago, a couple were visiting the churchyard to inspect some graves. Upon looking up, they saw a man in an old-fashioned horse and cart travelling down the lane, which lies adjacent to the church grounds. He was wearing a straw hat and smock, and he waved to them as the cart trundled past. The couple went into the lane for a closer look, only to find that the horse, cart, and driver had vanished into thin air.

Greyfriars Priory dates from the 13th century and is home to several ghostly monks. Lights have been seen, and the sounds of chanting have been heard. The legendary Black Shuck, the Devil Hound of East Anglia, was also observed running through the ruins in 1926. The witness claimed that it possessed glowing red eyes.

The Leper Chapel (John West).

Greyfriars Priory (John West).

The last surviving fragment of All Saint's Church (John West).

Willo-the-Wisps, known locally as Hobby Lanterns, were once thought to linger near the ruins of the priory. They would try to lure people over the edge of the cliffs to their deaths. These dancing lights were supposedly most active at night between September 29 and December 24.

The woodland path and the heath adjoining the cliffs are haunted by the brother of a long-forgotten lord of the manor. He fell in love with a serving girl who worked at the priory. Due to her lowly birth, he was forbidden by his brother from seeing her again and eventually died of a broken heart. In 2011, a couple claimed to have witnessed a pair of disembodied legs following them along the path before vanishing behind a tree. The legs were covered in dark trousers and boots. Paranormal researchers claim that his ghost is literally fading away, like a deteriorating video recording over the passage of time.

The heath is also home to another spirit, a former Victorian landowner named Barne, who still likes to ride his Arab racehorse across the fields whenever the moon is full. During the First World War, the ghostly horse and rider were seen by a squadron of Welsh cavalrymen billeted in a local house.

Chapter Nine

TRAVELLERS IN TIME?

THE VILLAGE

It was the summer of 1993, and Alf and Eileen Roberts were on their way home after a holiday. They were travelling through Devon towards a hotel in Dunster, Somerset, but found themselves lost. The couple stopped at a green to check their map but accidentally burned it with a cigarette. They then noticed a large varnished wooden sign in the middle of a flower bed, which read something like 'Award for the best kept village, Brampton, 1976.' Both were struck by the beauty of the surroundings and the vibrant colours of the flower beds, hanging baskets, and window box displays. They decided to drive on, taking note of the pink and orange paintwork of the stone cottages. They reached the end of the village but then decided to turn back. The couple saw an old man walking up the hill and asked him for directions. They then drove through an avenue of trees that had grown across the road. Although it was not yet dusk, it became so dark that Alf was forced to switch on his headlights as they drove away.

The couple decided to return to the village the following day to take some photographs. They were surprised to see that the sign and flower bed had vanished from the green – the area was now just grass. The village had also changed. The flower displays were gone, and even the colours of the houses were different. The walls were now a dull slate grey. To make matters even more mysterious, the burned map from the day before was not even damaged. Another unexplained problem was the time discrepancy. When they arrived in the village on the previous day, it was 7.30pm. The time on Alf's watch and the clock on the car dashboard still read 7.30pm when they left. When they retraced their journey the next day, it took 13 minutes to travel the same route. So what had happened to the lost 13 minutes? And had they briefly travelled back in time to 1976?

THE BATTLEFIELD

The bloody battle of Culloden Moor in 1746 finally ended any hope that a Stuart would sit again on the British throne. The site has long been reputed to be haunted, and many

An Incident in the Rebellion of 1745 by David Morier.

locals avoid the area on the anniversary of the battle for fear of seeing the ghosts of those who fell there so long ago.

In August 1949, Mr. and Mrs. Barton were visiting Scotland for the shooting and decided to visit the site. They followed the road that runs across the battlefield and examined the grave markers of the clansmen who had died there. Mrs. Barton then walked on, leaving her husband behind her. She came upon 'The Well of the Dead,' which lies in the centre of the battlefield. Suddenly, the sky turned grey, and a cold wind started blowing. She noticed several small thorn trees around the well. All were leafless and leaned away from the prevailing wind. Bloodstained rags – once white but now turned grey – fluttered in the breeze. A feeling of sadness filled the air.

Suddenly, the sunshine returned, and all was as it had been before. Her husband had apparently noticed nothing unusual, so she decided to keep the experience to herself. Two years passed, and the couple returned to Scotland. Mrs. Barton now told her husband about her vision, and both were keen to revisit the well. Upon reaching it, the pair saw that the thorn trees were gone and brambles now grew there instead. Mrs. Barton could only wonder at what had occurred to her before. Had she briefly seen the well in the immediate aftermath of battle? And were the bloodstained rags stained with the blood of the fallen from that terrible day in 1746?

Another interesting time slip connected with Culloden dates from May 29, 1973. Anne May and her husband were visiting Clava Cairns, an early Bronze Age burial site surrounded by birch trees about a mile from the battlefield. The lady practised yoga and lent against a stone of the north-eastern cairn. She emptied her mind of all thought, closed

The Well of the Dead, Culloden (Figgis-West).

her eyes, and then reopened them. She suddenly saw a group of men in tunics made of animal skin. Their hair was long, and they wore dark grey, cross-gartered trousers. They were pulling a large stone monolith across the ground. In the distance were the sounds of confused, muffled shouting. The vision vanished as a group of tourists entered the glade.

THE ISLAND

On January 4, 1969, Shelia White and her husband, a doctor, set off from St. Helens on the Isle of Wight to visit some friends in Niton. The night was cloudy and dark, and a large moon illuminated the fields. As the car crossed the Downs, the couple saw a large number of lights bobbing about in the fields to the right of them. It appeared as though people were carrying them, and the couple assumed that they were shepherds as it was the time for lambing. They reached the top of a hill, and the couple saw fields lit up 'like a great city.' They stopped the car and tried to figure out what they were seeing. They assumed the lights were part of an agricultural exhibition. Before them, a wide and brilliantly lit street led to buildings illuminated in green, orange, and red lights. The couple then realised that what they were seeing was superimposed on a cart track that led to a farmhouse.

The scene then vanished, and the area was plunged into darkness again. No lights were visible, and the quiet countryside seemed to have an air of menace about it. Now both scared, they got back into the car and drove on to the Hare and Hounds, a pub at the Newport and Merstone crossroads, to find someone who could explain what they had just witnessed. The pub was bathed in light and surrounded by figures carrying blazing torches. They were running backward and forward across the road. No sounds accompanied them. One of the figures was a very tall man with a dark complexion. He was wearing a broad-belted leather jerkin and ran in front of their car. The fields were also brightly lit, and this wash of light appeared to stretch into the distance towards Newport. Mrs. White was determined to stop and ask them what was happening, but when the car was about 20 yards from the pub, the lights and figures vanished. The pub was now in darkness, apart from some lights at the windows. The couple became scared again and drove off, not stopping until they reached Niton.

Mr. and Mrs. White returned to the area in the early morning, but all appeared normal. The towering clouds and oppressive atmosphere were gone.

Mrs. White later wondered if the running figures carrying torches were from the island's past. Were they Romans or Vikings? Both had occupied the island. The Vikings had also used it as a base to attack the mainland. And what of the fantastically coloured city? Had she been offered a glimpse into the far future, when a city stretched across a large part of what had once been open fields and woods?

THE FAIR

In October 1916, Edith Olivier, a superintendent in the Women's Land Army, was driving at dusk towards Avebury Stone Circle. The time was between five and six o'clock on what she described as 'a wet, dreary night.' She left the road and found herself entering an

Avebury (Jason Figgis).

avenue of huge grey stones. It was now raining, but Edith decided to park her car and explore the area. As she neared the ancient circle, she saw what appeared to be a large fair in the circle itself.

Edith later described what she saw: 'The grand megaliths and the humble cottages alike were partly obscured by the failing light and the falling rain, but both were fitfully lit by flares and torches from booths and shows. Some rather primitive swing boats flew in and out of this dim circle of light; coconuts rolled hairily from the sticks on which they had been planted; bottles were shivered by gunshots and tinkled as they fell to the ground. And all the time the little casual crowd of villagers strayed with true Wiltshire indifference from one sight to another, those great stones, the legacy of architects of an unknown race, had succeeded in adapting themselves completely to the village of another day. I stood on the bank for a short time watching the scene, and then I decided that too much rain was falling down the back of my neck, so I got into the car and drove away.'

It was about nine years before she returned to Avebury with a friend. A guidebook was consulted, and it emerged that the last fair held there was in 1850. She again visited Avebury the following year, this time as a member of a group studying the great prehistoric structure. She told her colleagues about the fair and the great avenue that she had walked along. One of those present then explained that the avenue had vanished before the early 1800s.

THE ROMAN TOWN

The remains of the Roman town of Verulamium lie in parkland and fields below the modern city of St. Albans. In the early 1950s, a certain Mr. B was visiting the site with two student teachers. They were viewing the scanty remains of the London Gate when Mr. B saw the gate suddenly become whole again. A small white chariot drawn by two cream Welsh ponies emerged from the gate, their speed increased by the whip of a young man wearing a belted tunic made of some fine material. The chariot drew level with Mr.B, and the ponies appeared to catch sight of him. They stopped sharply, digging their hooves into the ground. The young man did not appear to see him and lashed out, appearing to shout at the ponies (Mr. B could hear no sound) in an attempt to make them carry on. The vision only lasted a few seconds. His companions had seen nothing but had noticed that he looked 'strange' during his vision.

Another time slip connected with Verulamium concerns Mrs. Rawlings of Barnet in North London. She was visiting the ruined Roman theatre when she saw a procession of soldiers and standard bearers entering the arena. The last person to enter was a man dressed in white with a laurel wreath on his head. He sat down on a chair in the middle of a platform. Two standard bearers, each wearing an eagle insignia, then stood on either side of him. The image then faded away.

The Roman Theatre of Verulamium, St Albans (John West).

THE SHOP

In 1973, Mr. Squirrel, an elderly coin collector, was visiting Great Yarmouth in the county of Norfolk. He had been told of a shop – John Buckle Printers and Stationers, later demolished to make way for the Market Gates shopping centre – that sold small envelopes suitable for holding coins. He soon found the shop, noting the cobbled space in front and the brightly painted façade as he entered. The interior looked new but appeared very old-fashioned, with oilcloth covering the floor, framed floral pictures on the counter, a container of coloured walking sticks, and even an antique till. A female sales assistant in her early 30s appeared, and he noted her long, Edwardian-style black skirt, cameo brooch, and blouse with mutton-chop sleeves. Her old-fashioned look even extended to her hair, which was tied up in a bun.

He was not too surprised by her mode of dress, as many women at that time were wearing dresses that harked back in style to earlier decades. He asked her if the shop stocked envelopes for coins, and the lady gave him some from a foot-long brown box. She explained that they were in great demand by the men on the 'sailing ships,' who used them for holding fish hooks. Mr. Squirrel selected three dozen envelopes and was informed by the sales assistant that his purchases came to a shilling. He thought little of this, as decimalization had only occurred two years before and many still used pre-decimal terms to describe the new coinage. He gave her a 5p piece and noticed how she looked in astonishment at the coin. Despite her evident surprise, she put the envelopes in a brown bag that carried the shop's name.

Mr. Squirrel left but not before noting that the shop had been in total silence – even the sounds of traffic from outside had failed to penetrate the walls of the building. He related his strange experience to a friend, Miss Camm, and said he would shortly return to the shop for some more envelopes, as they had been so cheap.

A week later, he found himself standing outside the shop and was surprised to see how much it had altered since his first visit. The cobbles had been replaced with paving stones, and the exterior paintwork looked faded. The interior had also changed and now appeared 'dark and weathered.' There was also no sign of the framed photos, walking sticks, or even the old till. The assistant was now a lady in her 50s who claimed no knowledge of the younger woman who had served him a week ago. 'What, young lady? I am the only assistant here, and I've worked here for several years,' she said, adding, 'We have never had a lady assistant.' His request for more envelopes was met with the assurance that the shop had never stocked them. The manager also confirmed this and said that the shop's interior had not changed since his first visit a week before.

It is hardly surprising that the coin collector emerged from the building somewhat shaken but still firm in the knowledge that he was not mistaken about the location of the

Town Hall & Quay, Gt. Yarmouth.

shop or the reality of his first trip due to the evidence in the form of the paper bag and envelopes. Miss Camm later recalled how her elderly friend looked as 'white as a sheet' when he told her of what had happened on his second visit to the shop. The lady decided to contact Joan Forman, an author of books on the paranormal who was working on a publication devoted to time slips entitled *The Mask of Time*. It was hoped that she may be able to provide some help regarding the strange affair.

Miss Forman interviewed both Mr. Squirrel and Miss Camm and came away convinced of their sincerity. She asked to see the paper bag and envelopes, but was told that the bag had fallen to pieces after just a few days. The envelopes had also aged rapidly and had turned brown, but fortunately, the man had kept some of them. She decided to do some research on the envelopes and contacted the manufacturer to see if they still made them. They sent her the following reply: 'We have examined the transparent bag, and it would appear to have been made on one of our machines, as it closely resembles a standard line … Your specimen bag is made from Cellulose film, which, as you know, is produced from regenerated wood pulp.

'It is difficult to put an exact age on the bag, ... we think it is about 10 to 15 years old; after that period, Cellulose film becomes very brittle and is inclined to disintegrate when handled.

'Cellulose film came into use in the 1920s, although the method of manufacture was perfected before the First World War.'

Joan was puzzled by the case but felt that the existence of the envelopes ruled out a genuine time slip, as they couldn't be accurately tied in with the Edwardian style of the shop or the lady's appearance.

Although I respect Miss Forman's findings, I am afraid I must disagree with her. I have seen photographs of English ladies taken in 1920 who are clearly still wearing Edwardian-style dresses. So had Mr. Squirrel found himself in the 1920s rather than a year predating 1914?

The age of the envelopes – 10 to 15 years – was also based on the way they had aged rather than the date of manufacture. And how are we going to explain their rapid deterioration over just a few days when such ageing should take at least 10 years?

So what really happened to Mr. Squirrel? He did offer one possible explanation. His grandfather was also a Norfolk man and had been interested in coins. Had he carried a genetic memory of his grandfather visiting the shop, and did his visit there trigger a replay of this in his mind? It is an interesting theory, but one that would not explain the physical evidence of the envelopes.

I am inclined to think that Mr. Squirrel really did find himself briefly interacting with someone from another time, as did the others in this chapter. They were certainly not alone in suddenly finding themselves in the past, as readers of *An Adventure* by Charlotte Anne Moberly and Eleanor Jourdain may recall. Their book describes a visit they made to the Petit Trianon, a small château in the grounds of the Palace of Versailles, where they claimed to have seen the gardens as they had appeared in the late 18th century, as well as several people, including a person they believed to be Marie Antoinette. A further example of a time slip took place in 1996, when a man walking down Bold Street in Liverpool suddenly found himself surrounded by people and cars apparently dating back in style to the 1950s or early 1960s. As he entered a shop, the scene suddenly reverted to the present.

I also had an interesting experience in the 1980s during a visit to Blackfriars Priory in Hereford. As I walked around the ruins, the sounds of nearby school children playing and the noise of traffic started to fade away, and the building no longer appeared to be a ruin. The feeling only lasted for a few seconds before the sounds of the 20th century returned and the building reverted to its ruined state.

The factors that trigger a time slip cannot yet be determined, but Albert Einstein was clearly on to something when he said, 'People like us, who believe in physics, know that the distinction between past, present, and future is only a stubbornly persistent illusion.'

Chapter Ten

THE CURSE OF THE PICKERING

The *Pickering*, a 65ft-long trawler, was part of the fishing fleet that sailed from the port of Bridlington in Yorkshire. She had been built in 1975 in the shipyards of Cork, Ireland, and originally bore the name *Family Crest.* One day in December, the vessel was off the coast of County Mayo with another trawler. A net had been cast into the sea, and as it was being pulled in, three of the crew became caught in it and were pulled overboard into the freezing waters. Two of the men were saved, but the third was lost. His body was never found.

The owner, Jimmy O'Donnell, decided to give up fishing and sell the vessel after the tragedy. She was sold to Michael Barker, who owned a fishing fleet in Yorkshire. He renamed her *Pickering*. Some seamen believe that renaming a ship brings back luck. This superstition goes back a long time and is mentioned in the classic novel *Treasure Island*, in which Long John Silver is recorded as saying, 'What a ship was christened, so let her stay.' Perhaps the new owner should have heeded this warning.

The new skipper of the *Pickering* was Mick Laws. He had been excited about his new job but soon changed his mind as the vessel was plagued with mechanical faults. The mate, John Jarvis, later recalled the problems they experienced. The autopilot would fail, and lights would flicker on and off in the wheelhouse. The boat would be repaired, and it would again head out to sea. Within minutes, further problems would arise, and they would be forced to return to port. Things got so bad that the crew was not even covering their expenses.

Chris Clark, a senior engineer working for a company that serviced the fleet, recalled going to the vessel and being unable to pin down a reason for the constant electrical failures. For instance, the autopilot would be asked to go to port but would go to starboard. He changed the wires around, and this appeared to rectify the problem. However, within a day, the autopilot was up to its old tricks again. Mr. Clark returned to the vessel and was amazed at what he discovered. The polarity going to the two wires had been reversed. This was against the laws of physics. He was forced to reverse the wires.

Other things were happening on board too. There was a strange atmosphere on the ship. The cabin was always cold, and the installation of a new heating system failed to

Bridlington Harbour (Figgis-West).

solve the problem. Mr. Jarvis recalled how the fish room, with eight tons of ice, was still warmer than the cabin. The captain also had a strange experience as he got into his bunk. The side of the mattress went down as if someone were climbing into the bunk above him. He called out 'Hello,' but no one answered. He laid back, and the mattress did the same thing again. He jumped up and searched the cabin. He was alone. The mattress went down again, and the captain rushed into the mess room and asked if any of them had been in the cabin. None of them had.

Stories circulated that a name was scratched into the bunk, and it was thought the name was of the man who had drowned. Things became so bad that Mr. Jarvis decided to leave the ship.

One night at sea, one of the crewmen, Barry Mason, rushed into the mess room, terrified. He said he had seen a shadowy figure on deck. They all ran up on deck but could find no one.

In 1987, the six-man crew was forced to claim unemployment benefits because the trawler was not making money. An investigator, William Buckley, was told that as soon as the boat left port, something took over the steering mechanism, causing it to go around in circles. Coastguard officers confirmed his story. It was concluded that the men had sufficient grounds for claiming benefits. The captain expressed his frustration to the clerk at the Bridlington Job Centre and said that he was thinking of looking for an exorcist.

The clerk called over his manager, James Trowsdale. James was a lay reader at a local church and offered to help. He arranged for the captain to meet the Rev. Tom Willis, who was a parish priest and an exorcist. Mr. Willis was also one of nine advisers to the Archbishop of York on occult disturbances.

Mr. Willis talked to Mick Laws and another captain who had been in charge of the trawler. He looked into the history of the vessel and learned of the death of the seaman off the coast of Ireland. Mr. Willis felt that the man's spirit was unable to move on after being denied a proper burial. It was decided to exorcise the *Pickering*.

The day of the exorcism soon arrived. Mr. Willis was joined by Mr. Trowsdale, who was to act as an observer. The pair travelled to Bridlington and found themselves being offered a lift by Chris Clark, the engineer, who was being called out to fix yet another electrical fault on the boat. Mr. Laws welcomed them all aboard. It was suggested that the vessel be put to sea to deter undue attention from the public or press. Mr. Willis, dressed in a cassock and purple sash, then proceeded to sprinkle holy water around the boat. He commanded all evil to depart and asked that 'peace be unto this ship and all who sail in her.' He then suggested that the crew gather on the deck and pray.

The next day, Mr. Willis called the captain. Everything was now running smoothly, and the cold spots and sense of evil had vanished. However, this new-found peace was to prove short-lived.

A new skipper, John Hilton, took charge of the vessel and found that strange things continued to happen onboard. A sonar screen once came on by itself during one of the voyages. When the captain went below decks to discover the reason behind it, he found that the power to the screen had been disconnected. This would have made it impossible for the screen to operate. The sound of someone climbing down the metal ladder was also heard. Once, when the *Pickering* was tied to the dock, the captain heard loud bangs coming from the now-deserted ship. He described the sound as like a hammer hitting a metal pipe. A search failed to turn up an explanation for the disturbance. The vessel continued to be plagued by bad luck and electrical faults. The captain and the crew finally decided to leave what they now regarded as an unlucky ship. The vessel was abandoned and eventually sold for scrap.

Chapter Eleven

THE PHANTOMS
OF MUNCASTER CASTLE

Muncaster Castle overlooks the River Esk in Cumbria and is believed to stand on the site of a Roman fort. The oldest parts of the building date from the 14th century, including the Great Hall and a pele tower, a type of watch tower that is unique to the English-Scottish border area. The castle was heavily remodelled in the 1860s by the architect Anthony Salvin on behalf of the Barons Muncaster.

Today, Muncaster is owned by the Pennington family, who have held the land for some 800 years. They also share the castle with several ghosts and a lucky talisman.

The famous 'Luck of Muncaster' is a glass drinking bowl that was supposedly given to Sir John Pennington by Henry VI after the Battle of Towton in 1461. The King fled to the castle and gave Sir John the bowl in gratitude for his help. He also hoped that the family would prosper so long as it remained unbroken.

A 600-year-old chestnut tree in the castle grounds is associated with Muncaster's most famous ghost, Tom Skelton. Tom was the castle's steward and jester in the 16th century. He acquired the nickname 'Tom Fool,' and the term 'tomfoolery' owes its origin to him. He is said to have known Shakespeare and been the model for King Lear's fool. Tom may have been a jester, but he also had an evil streak. He would sit underneath the chestnut tree, where he would be asked for directions by travellers on the road. If he liked them, he would point to a nearby ford. If he did not like the look of them, he would send them into the quicksands of the River Esk and almost certain death.

Skelton was also involved in a brutal murder. Helwise, the daughter of Sir William Pennington, had fallen in love with Richard, the son of a carpenter, despite being promised to the son of a powerful neighbouring family. Sir William found out and told Tom to put an end to the affair; another version of the story claims that the rejected suitor paid Tom to kill his rival. Tom was more than happy to do so, as he believed that the young man had stolen money from him. One version of the story says that he lured the carpenter to the castle with the claim that he would meet his lover. Richard was surprised to find Tom

Tom Skelton, the murderous fool of Muncaster Castle.

waiting for him, but the jester offered him several drinks with the promise that his love would soon join them. The carpenter quickly became insensible, and Tom decapitated him with an axe. He then boasted to the servants, 'I have hidden Dick's head under a heap of shavings, and he will not find that so easily when he awakes, as he did my shillings.'

Muncaster Castle in the 1880s.

After the murder, Sir William's daughter joined a nunnery, spending the rest of her days longing for her murdered lover. Tom Skelton never paid for his crime, but sometimes fate has a way of punishing the wrongdoer – he is thought to have drowned in the River Esk. His ghost is said to walk the castle grounds, and the sounds of thuds on the stairs are thought by some to be the sounds of Skelton dragging the carpenter's headless body to show his master.

The Tapestry Room is one of the most active spots in the castle. It has a bad atmosphere, with women appearing to be most affected. Some have even refused to enter the room. Others also feel that they are being watched upon entering it. Alan Clark, the garden curator, slept in an adjoining room and found that the large wooden doors opened twice on their own. The late Lord Carlisle had once stayed in the Tapestry Room and thought it a very unpleasant place. He refused to ever stay in the room again after he was woken up in the night and heard a baby crying for ten minutes. He was unable to trace the source of the cries.

James Cartland, a friend of the Pennington family, visited the castle in the 1980s and found himself staying in the Tapestry Room. He was reading some letters when he heard someone muttering. It sounded like a child, and then he heard another person enter the room. This person was then heard talking to the child and trying to calm it down. Cartland searched the room, even checking the chimney to see if the wind was responsible for the sounds. However, there was no wind. It was a clear and frosty night, and no one else was staying in that part of the castle.

The next morning, he told the other guests what had happened. One of them then phoned her daughter, who told him of her experience in the very same room. It had happened a year before. She was in bed when she suddenly felt that someone was with her. Footsteps could be heard outside, and the door opened slightly. More footsteps and the sounds of children talking were then heard. The children began chanting or singing, which terrified the woman.

A corridor in the castle is also haunted. A former curator, Philip Denham-Cookes, was walking along it when he saw a woman with her back to him. Her hair was tied in a bun, and she was wearing what looked like a coffee-coloured negligée. He assumed that she was a member of the public who was lost and had been shut in the castle by mistake. She then appeared to walk through a locked door. He later spoke to the then-current owner, Sir William Pennington, about what he had seen. It emerged that Sir William's mother had often worn a coffee-coloured negligee and had her hair tied in exactly the same way as the phantom.

One female tourist was standing in the corridor, looking at the forbidding portrait of Tom Skelton. She heard someone walking on the stone floor behind her and started to comment on the painting, assuming that another visitor was behind her. She received no answer and, on turning around, discovered that no one was there. She then realised that the corridor was carpeted.

The partner of a member of staff once saw a man in 15th-century clothing. It was during the day, and she said hello to him as they passed one another. She turned back to take another glance at the man and found that he had vanished. She assumed that he was part of a film crew and had walked into the other courtyard. However, a search of the castle failed to find him.

Clifford Jones, an archaeologist, was visiting the castle as part of his research into the Roman occupation of the area. He was staying in one of the castle towers when he heard wood being chopped outside. He went down into the courtyard and called out for the chopping to cease. The sounds stopped, and he suddenly realised that only he and the mistress of the castle were staying there at the time, and she was nowhere near the courtyard. Scared, he ran upstairs and into the bathroom. As he did so, the bulb blew. He went back to the landing, and the bulb blew there too. He then went into the lounge, and the bulbs in that room also failed. He was so scared by this experience that he left the castle for three days.

The King's Room is also haunted. Patrick Gordon-Duff-Pennington went to go into the room one morning, and something pulled the door from the other side as he opened it. One winter, he also found himself being followed by footsteps every evening after leaving the tearoom to walk to his office.

The Association for the Scientific Study of Anomalous Phenomena (ASSAP) was impressed by these stories and decided to investigate the haunting. In April 1994, Jason Braithwaite and his team spent a night at the castle. At 2.45am, Ian Topham was in the Tapestry Room when he saw a dark figure walk through a door and then pause. It had no features and vanished as it neared him.

Another team member, Melanie Warren, was in the King's Room when she witnessed a shadowy figure going into the Tapestry Room. She thought it was a fellow team member. She followed it but found Ian alone. Of the other figure, there was no sign.

It turned out that the Tapestry Room was used as a nursery in the 19th century. It emerged that a girl, Margaret Susan Elizabeth Pennington, the daughter of the fourth Lord Muncaster, had died in 1871. She was only 11 and had screaming fits before she died. It is believed that she slept in the Tapestry Room. Was she responsible for the strange happenings there?

The actor Robert Hardy made a documentary series on haunted castles in the 1990s and visited Muncaster to film there. In the documentary, he tells of another paranormal investigation held at the castle in September 1993. The experts had set up an array of monitoring equipment and, at 10.40pm, felt the temperature drop dramatically. A vase then began to shake, and a thud was heard. This was followed by three raps, and the shadow of something moving in another room was seen at the bottom of a door. The paranormal team concluded that the castle was haunted.

Mr. Hardy also discovered that the road leading to Muncaster had a ghost. He spoke to Grace Simmons, an employee of the castle, who said that one night in October 1995, she had been driving with her husband along the road when she saw a distressed woman in white leaning against a wall. She asked her husband to stop the car, as she wanted to see if the lady was all right. Grace got out but found that the woman had vanished.

The woman in white is linked to a gruesome murder in the early 1800s. Mary Bragg, a housekeeper in Ravenglass, was in love with a member of the castle staff. However, the housekeeper of the castle was also in love with the man and was determined to get rid of her rival. One night, two men arrived at Mary's door, claiming that her beloved was ill. She joined them but never made it to her lover's side. The men suddenly pulled Mary from the carriage in which they were travelling and dragged her to a tree, where they shot her. They left her body in the castle grounds for the dogs to devour, but when that failed, they took her body to the river and threw it in. Months later, it was found washed up on the river bank. An inquest was held, and a doctor stated that it was impossible to determine the cause of death – some say that he was bribed to cover up the murder. But those involved in Mary's death did not escape justice. One went insane, and another was executed for highway robbery. Mary's rival did not prosper either. She was shunned by the locals as a suspected murderess and finally left the castle. Even the doctor did not escape. He was found drowned in the River Esk, not 100 yards from where Mary's body had been first dumped.

In 1993, the tree under which Mary died was cut down. The timber was said to be cursed. Blood was seen to drip from the cut wood, and no one locally would have anything to do with it. The timber finally had to be shipped to London to be sold.

The spirit of Mary Bragg is still said to linger at the spot where the tree once stood.

Chapter Twelve

CAPITAL GHOSTS

L ondon's history stretches back some 2,000 years. Romans, Saxons, Vikings, and Normans all settled there. The city has seen torture, executions, plague, fire, and destruction from the air in two world wars. With such a bloody history, it is hardly surprising to learn that London is also a very haunted city. Indeed, some claim it to be the most haunted place in the world. Read on and discover some of the many tales from London's ghostly past.

NEWGATE PRISON

Old Newgate Prison has long since been demolished. It was a very haunted building, and many strange things were witnessed there over the years. In December 1891, a prison officer was working late in his office when he heard limping footsteps coming from Dead Man's Walk, a long, stone-flagged passageway where the bodies of executed criminals were buried.

Newgate Prison in the 19th century.

Newgate Prison Chapel.

The officer thought it was the chief warder making his rounds, but then realised the sounds were very different from the measured, military step of his colleague. The officer opened the grill in the door, which led to Dead Man's Walk, and saw the deathly white face of a man looking back at him. The figure swayed back from the door, and the officer saw bruises on the man's mottled green throat. He looked as if he had been hanged. The face then vanished, and a search of the area found no one. Others later heard the same limping footsteps, and it emerged that the last executed prisoner buried in Dead Man's Walk was lame.

Thurston Hopkins, the Sussex writer and ghost hunter, once wrote of a prison chaplain who was alone in the chapel when he saw the black curtains of the condemned pew swish back to reveal a gaunt-faced man with powdered hair and a black coat. The chaplain later saw a portrait of Henry Fauntleroy, a banker who had been executed for forgery in 1824, and recognised him as the man that he had seen in the chapel.

Amelia Dyer

115

Newgate Prison cell door

The notorious murderess, Amelia Elizabeth Dyer, haunted the Women's Felon's Yard. She had been arrested in 1896 for killing babies that she had been paid to adopt. It is believed that she murdered some 400 infants during her murderous career, making her one of the most prolific serial killers in history. Such was her callous nature that she even smiled at the trial as the details of her crimes were read out to the shocked court. It is hardly surprising to learn that she was sentenced to death. As she walked to the scaffold, she looked at Mr. Scot, the chief warder. and said, 'I'll meet you again someday, sir.'

In 1902, the prison was due to close. It was the last week, and the chief warder found himself with some of his fellow warders in the keeper's room next to the Women's Felons Yard. He suddenly felt as if someone was looking at him, and Mrs. Dyer's last words to him started to ring in his head: 'Meet you again. Meet you again.' He looked towards the door that led to the yard and saw, through a glass observation panel, a sad-looking face staring at him. It was Amelia Dyer. She had kept her vow.

A prison official and his wife were sitting in their kitchen the night before the deserted prison was due to be demolished. They had just finished their supper when the bell in the condemned cell started to ring. The man went to investigate and found the cell empty. The bell was still gently swinging.

THE MURDER OF WILLIAM TERRISS

The Adelphi Theatre is haunted by the actor William Terriss, who was stabbed to death there by a jealous rival. Terriss was one of Victorian England's most popular actors, with a string of successful roles to his name.

Terriss had earned the hatred of a mentally unstable actor called Richard Archer Prince. He had helped his colleague find work in various productions, but during the run of *The Harbour Lights*, Terriss was angered by something that Prince had said about him, and the actor was removed from the cast. Despite this, Terriss sent small sums of money to Prince via the Actors' Benevolent Fund and also tried to find him roles. By December 1897, Prince's alcoholism and mental instability had worsened, and he had no money and no work.

On December 14, 1897, Terriss was heard arguing with Prince in his dressing room at the Adelphi Theatre. On December 16, Prince asked for money at the fund's office but was turned down. He then crossed the street and hid in a doorway near the Adelphi's stage door. When his hated rival arrived for an evening performance, Prince attacked Terriss, stabbing him three times with a knife. Prince later told police, 'I did it for revenge. He had kept me out of employment for ten years, and I had either to die in the street or kill him. '

Terriss collapsed just inside the stage door and was carried inside. He died 20 minutes later, comforted by his leading lady, Jessie Millward. Just as he was about to die, he is said to have mumbled, 'I will come back.'

Prince was declared mad and spent the rest of his life in Broadmoor, where he organised plays and other entertainments for his fellow inmates. He died in 1937 at the age of 79.

It is interesting to note that the day before the murder, Frederick Lane, who was Terriss's understudy, had come to the theatre and spoke of a terrible dream he had the previous night. In the dream, Terriss was lying unconscious on the stairs leading to the theatre's dressing rooms. Blood was streaming from a wound in his chest. Three witnesses later signed affidavits stating that Lane had told them of his dream before the murder occurred.

The murder of William Terriss as depicted in the Illustrated Police News.

It was not long after the murder that strange things began to happen at the Adelphi. Taps and raps were heard coming from Terriss's dressing room. In the years that followed, unexplained footsteps, lights, and noises were also heard in the theatre at night. The feeling of being watched was reported, and many felt that Terriss's ghost was responsible for the odd happenings.

THE BLOOD STAINED KNIFE
(EXACT SIZE)

MR. J.H. GRAVES. WHO WITNESSED THE MURDER.

181 E

POLICE CONSTABLE BRAGG. 272. E.

THE MAGISTRATE EXAMINES THE FATAL KNIFE

SERGEANT BUSH.

PRISONER

PRISONERS ONLY

THE MURDERER LOUDLY HISSED ON LEAVING THE DOCK AT BOW STREET

The trial of Prince as depicted in the Illustrated Police News.

In March 1928, a musical comedy actress was using the dressing room formally occupied by Jessie Millward. She was resting on a couch when it began to vibrate as if someone were kicking it. She looked underneath the couch but could find no reason for the movement. She got back on the couch, and it started moving again. The actress also experienced light blows on her arm. She then felt her arm being gripped by someone and

The Aldephi Theatre.

saw a green glow in the dressing table mirror. She got up and put out her hand towards the light. The light vanished, and she noticed red marks on her arm where she had been held. A couple of taps were then heard, and these appeared to come from behind the mirror.

The actress told her dresser, Ethel Rollin, what had happened. The dresser told her about the alleged haunting and said that she often heard a couple of taps on the door of the dressing room after the actress had left to go on stage. She would check the dressing room but always found it empty. It was then remembered that Terriss would always tap twice on the dressing room door of his leading lady to let her know that he had arrived. A séance was held in the dressing room, attended by famed psychic investigator and author Harry Price, but nothing happened. However, for several months after this, no taps or sounds were heard coming from the haunted room.

One summer evening in 1957, a visitor to London saw a figure dressed in old-fashioned clothes vanish at the spot where Terriss had been attacked. In 1962, two members of the Adelphi staff saw a similar light to the one seen in 1928. The theatre was closed, and the stage was only lit by two pilot lights. One of the stagehands suddenly became very cold as a light appeared on the stage. It floated just above the stage and appeared to be shaped like a human figure. The other stagehand saw it too, and they both fled the building. They asked the manager to be transferred to another part of the theatre. He was unimpressed by their request and explained that it was just the harmless ghost of William Terriss. The

William Terriss.

men changed their minds after hearing this and carried on working in their old positions.

An electrician was working alone one night on the stage. He was standing at the top of a pair of step ladders when the velvet curtains covering the exit parted and a grey-suited man appeared from nowhere. He then mounted the stairs and walked up to the stalls. The electrician ran up the parallel flight of stairs to catch him as he mounted the next flight of steps to the circle. He reached the top, but the man had vanished. He flashed his torch across the rows of seats but could see nothing. As he turned to walk back to find the theatre's fireman, he heard a noise. Seats began to flip up as if someone were walking along the rows towards a door marked 'Exit'.

In 1973, the actor Peter Wyngarde of *Jason King* fame was using the star dressing room during a run of *The King and I*. Objects kept vanishing after being put down. Peter would then ask the ghost to return them, and the objects would suddenly reappear in a place that had previously been searched. The actor also mentioned to the press that his dresser, David Lewis, had once seen a man in old-fashioned clothes in the wardrobe area.

In 2013, the comedian Jason Manford was using the haunted dressing room. He was chatting with his three-year-old daughter on Skype when she suddenly asked who the man standing behind him was. Manford was alone in the dressing room, and he asked his daughter what the man looked like. She replied that he looked like a soldier. It is interesting to note that William Terriss's last role at the Adelphi was playing an American Civil War captain.

COVENT GARDEN UNDERGROUND STATION

William Terriss does not appear to have confined his appearances to the Adelphi. Peter Underwood, the author of many books on ghosts, learned that his spirit also haunted the nearby tube station. Although not in existence at the time of Terriss's death, the station did stand on the site of a bakery once used by the actor. Underwood interviewed the witnesses in 1955 and found that for three years, staff working on the line had seen a figure in one of the tunnels after the station had closed for the day. The sounds of footsteps, gasps, sighs, and loud bangs were also heard.

Jack Hayden was the foreman ticket collector. He told Underwood that after locking all the gates, he went to the platform to check that the place was empty. He noticed a tall and distinguished-looking man walking along the westbound subway. He was then seen climbing the emergency spiral stairs. Hayden telephoned the booking office and told the clerk to stop the man when he reached the top. He then took the lift to meet his colleague, who told him that no one had emerged from the stairway. Both men searched the stairs and the station but could find no trace of the man.

A few days went by, and Hayden was eating in the staff mess room. It was after midnight, and the last train had gone. The door suddenly opened, and he saw the same man standing before him. He described the man as wearing a grey suit, an old-style shirt collar, a curly-brimmed hat, and light-coloured gloves. He asked what he wanted, but the man did not answer and walked off. Hayden got up and looked through the door into the passage. The man had vanished.

Four days later, Hayden and a colleague were in the mess room. They heard a scream, and Victor Locker, a 19-year-old porter, rushed in. He had seen a strange-looking man standing in the corner of an adjacent room. He asked him what he was doing there. As

Covent Garden Station.

he did so, he suddenly felt something pressing down on his head. The man then vanished into thin air. He added that the man was wearing 'funny-looking clothes' and light-coloured gloves (Terriss always wore light-coloured gloves). Hayden then described his own sighting, and Locker said it matched the description of the figure he had just seen. The porter was so shocked by his experience that he requested a transfer to another station. Hayden was later shown a photograph of William Terriss. He recognised him as the man he had first seen on the platform.

Underwood also interviewed Eric Davey, a foreman at Leicester Square station, who said that he was clairvoyant and had become aware of an unseen presence in the mess room at Covent Garden station. He said that the spirit was trying to say a name that began with the letters 'Ter .'

Hayden told Underwood that Terriss was seen in November and December. He always wore the same clothes and usually appeared near a wall. Hayden had tried to speak to him, but Terriss had never replied. The last time he had seen the ghost was in November

1964. He had been walking down the spiral staircase and had come face to face with the apparition climbing the same stairs. Scared, he rushed past the figure, who did not appear to be aware of him. Hayden left Covent Garden in 1965, as the thought of seeing Terriss again was becoming too much for him.

The ghost continued to appear after Hayden's departure and was often seen on Sundays, when the station was closed. Later witnesses included an engineer, a signalman, a stationmaster, and various other members of staff. The last recorded sighting of him was in 1972, when a lift operator, Christopher Joseph Clifford, was closing the station for the night. Something made him turn around, and he saw a tall man standing before him. He was wearing old-fashioned clothes and a tall hat. He assumed that he had accidentally locked the man in and reached over to get the keys to let him out. When he turned back, the man had vanished. A search of the stairs and the platforms failed to find him. A colleague later showed Clifford a photograph of William Terriss. It was the spitting image of the person he had seen.

It has now been over 50 years since the last sighting of Terriss. Has the actor finally moved on from this earthly stage to embrace a new role beyond the veil of death?

THE LYCEUM

The old Lyceum theatre was the scene of a strange haunting in the 1880s. A man was watching a performance there with his wife when he happened to look down from their box. He saw a richly dressed woman in the fourth row who had a man's head in her lap!

The Lyceum Theatre.

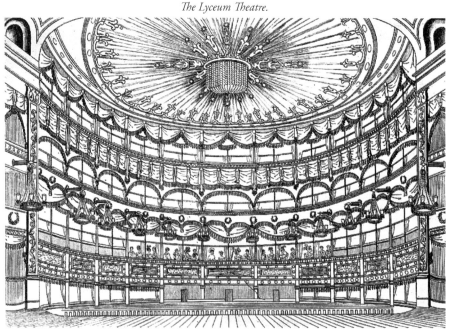

The wife noticed her husband looking down at the woman and asked what she had in her lap as it looked like a man's head. The head's eyes were closed, and it had long hair, a moustache, and a pointed beard.

At the intermission, the couple went down to try to get a closer look at the woman and the head. The object was now apparently hidden under the lady's silk wrap. They returned to their box, and at the end of the show, they tried to follow the woman but lost her in the crowds as she left the theatre.

A few years later, the man was visiting a hall in Yorkshire to value some of the paintings there. He saw the portrait of a bearded man. His face matched the features of the head he had seen at the Lyceum. He discovered that the painting was of an ancestor of the family at the hall who had been beheaded for treason. His family, the Courtenays, had owned the land on which the Lyceum now stands.

THE WARNING

The artist Mrs. P. Fitzgerald once rented a studio in a house in Red Lion Square. One night she was returning to it when she saw a shabbily dressed woman leave the building. As the woman walked by her, she hissed, 'Lady, don't paint the bridge.' Mrs. Fitzgerald looked back and found that she had vanished. Puzzled, she asked the owner of the house, Dr. Josiah Oldfield, about the woman. He appeared reluctant to discuss it but did say that he knew of no one matching her description.

A few days went by, and the artist was asked to paint a roof garden that had a bridge linking it to two floors. She had a bad feeling about the job and turned the offer down. She later heard that the bridge and part of the roof garden had collapsed on the very day that she would have been working there.

Several years later, Dr. Oldfield told Mrs. Fitzgerald of a gipsy woman who had been murdered by a mob after being accused of witchcraft. The crime had taken place in his home during the 1660s. Had her ghost been responsible for the warning?

CLEOPATRA'S NEEDLE

The ancient Egyptian obelisk known as Cleopatra's Needle, although dating from 1,000 years before her reign, has long been a magnet for suicides. Strange sounds like groans and mocking laughter have been heard there, and its sinister reputation is further enhanced by stories of a nude and shadowy figure that is seen to disappear over the parapet and vanish into the water without a sound.

A policeman was once crossing Waterloo Bridge in the early hours of the morning when he heard someone running after him. He turned around to see a well-dressed young lady who begged him to follow her as someone was in grave danger. She led him along the Embankment to Cleopatra's Needle, where he spotted a young woman about to throw

Cleopatra's Needle.

herself into the Thames. He dashed forward and grabbed her just as she was about to jump into the cold waters. He was shocked to see that the woman was the exact double of the person who had summoned him – even her dress was the same. He turned to speak to the other woman but found that she had vanished into thin air.

THE MURDER HOUSE

An unnamed house near the parish church in Hampstead was the scene of a terrifying murder that left a psychic trace in the property that lasted for well over 100 years. Strange sounds were often heard in the hall, something that was likened to a sigh and a shudder. The running footsteps of a child were also noted in various parts of the house. Sometimes they would stop suddenly and retreat slowly, as if the child had come face to face with something.

The sounds of someone slowly climbing the stairs and sighs in the upstairs rooms, especially at night, were also heard. September seemed to be the most active month. The phantom of a woman with red hair and holding a carpet bag was observed standing by the front door. She appeared to be breathing heavily, as if exhausted from some heavy labour. It emerged that the murder had been committed by a woman with red hair. She had killed and dismembered a child in the house. She had then carried the remains away in a carpet bag.

THE BUS

The 1930s saw a number of people in North Kensington report seeing a number seven double-decker bus racing down St. Mark's Road long after all scheduled bus services had ended for the day. Its lights were on, but there was no sign of a driver or a conductor. The bus was responsible for more than one near-fatal accident as cars were forced off the road in order to avoid it as it turned the corner of St. Mark's Road and Cambridge Gardens. The bus would then vanish.

A man once reported seeing a bus pull up at a garage late one night. No sound accompanied its appearance, and when he looked again, the bus had disappeared. A person who lived on St. Mark's Road, near the junction, told Peter Underwood that he and his wife had seen the empty bus at least six times. They would even stay up after midnight, waiting for the sound of yet another car's screeching brakes as it tried to avoid the phantom vehicle.

Another witness told Underwood that he was crossing St. Mark's Road when he saw a car veer off the road and mount the pavement. The man rushed over to the car, assuming that the driver had been taken ill. The man was very shaken and spoke of a bus that had come around the corner too fast and caused him to lose control. He then asked what had happened to it. Underwood's informant told the shocked man that he had not seen another vehicle, saying the road had been deserted but for his car.

In 1934, Ian James Steven Beaton was killed after hitting another car driven by the chauffeur of British peer Samuel Vestey. An inquest was held in Paddington, and a witness was asked if the accident had occurred at the spot where the phantom bus was said to appear. The witness confirmed that it had.

The junction of St. Mark's Road and Cambridge Gardens was a dangerous one, and it was finally decided to remove part of a private garden in order to make the corner safe.

After this was done, the bus was never seen again. Some later speculated that the bus had been sent as a warning of danger, and the alteration of the corner satisfied whatever had caused the ghostly vehicle to first appear.

THE ANGEL OF DEATH

Part of the old St. Thomas's Hospital in Lambeth was haunted by a Grey Lady. The ghost was described as being middle-aged and wearing a grey nurse's uniform. It was always seen in Block 8, a ward that specialised in malignant diseases.

In 1929, Edwin Frewer was the new superintendent of the hospital. He was walking along the main corridor with his superior, Mr. French, when he suddenly noticed a drop in the temperature. He then saw a nurse walking towards them from Block 8. She was wearing an old-fashioned uniform and a long skirt. She had a look of anguish on her face, but vanished as she neared them. The only exit was a door leading to a sleeping block, and that was firmly locked. Mr. French had not seen the nurse and had been surprised when Mr. Frewer had stopped for no apparent reason.

Mr. Frewer later discovered that one of the doctors, Dr. Anwyl-Davis, had seen the same woman in April 1937. She had appeared in the same corridor and disappeared at almost exactly the same spot. The doctor had raised his hat in greeting and wished her a good morning. The nurse appeared unaware of him and did not respond. She then vanished.

In November 1943, Charles Bide, a member of the hospital staff, was at the top of Block 8. A German bomb had damaged the hospital the previous night, and several windows had been blown out. Mr. Bide was in charge of the hospital clocks and was looking at the damage when he noticed an oil painting and a mirror left untouched by the bomb. He removed the painting from the wall and then turned his attention to the mirror. A woman of about 35 was now reflected in the glass. She was dressed in grey and looked troubled. A feeling of coldness suddenly overcame him, and he became scared and left the area. He

ST. THOMAS'S HOSPITAL ON THE ALBERT EMBANKMENT
OPENED BY HER MAJESTY JUNE 21, 1871

later regretted this, as he felt that the ghost had been trying to communicate with him and had meant him no harm. He later wondered if he could have helped her move on if he had stood his ground.

In September 1956, a nurse was filling the water jugs in a ward. The time was 8.30pm. She went to the bed of a man suffering from cancer, who told her that another nurse had already given him a glass of water. There was no other nurse on the ward, but the man insisted that a lady in grey was standing at the bottom of the bed. However, she could see no one. The man died two days later.

Two months went by, and another nurse was on duty in the same unit but in a different ward. She had been washing the back of a man of 70 who was very ill. He asked her about the other nurse and asked if she always worked with her. He then pointed to an empty part of the room where he said she was standing. He described her as being 'dressed differently' and mentioned that she often came to visit him. He died not long afterwards.

In December 1957, the ghost was again seen in the same ward. A cancer patient in his 30s asked the sister on duty about the other nurse warming her hands by the fire. No one was standing there, and the nurse asked him to describe her. He replied that she was dressed in grey. He died two days later.

In February 1958, a very ill patient told the night nurse about a lady in grey who had been very kind and had brought her a cup of tea. She died the very next day. A year later, another female patient in the very same ward told a nurse that she had seen the same figure standing at the foot of her bed one night. She had not been scared and described the woman as being very kind and sympathetic. This patient also died a few days later.

The apparition also appeared in another ward of the same unit a few years later. A nurse was on night duty and was called upon to supervise the giving of a dangerous drug to a terminally ill patient. The nurse asked the patient if she could make her more comfortable, only for the woman to reply that the other nurse had just helped her. No other nurse had attended to the lady, who died the next day.

The grey nurse's uniform described by the witnesses went out of use in the early 1920s. Some of the nurses also maintained that the apparition was only visible from the mid-calf upwards. This was thought to be due to the floor level having changed when the block was rebuilt. Four separate deaths have been offered as a possible explanation for the Grey Lady appearing in Block 8. In the early years of the last century, a nurse was said to have fallen down a lift shaft and been killed. Another nurse is supposed to have killed herself in her office on the top floor of Block 8. A third contender for the phantom is a nurse who died of smallpox, and a fourth concerns the sister who threw herself off a balcony in despair after accidentally causing the death of a patient. No records survive to confirm the details of these deaths, and so the identity of the mysterious Grey Lady must forever remain lost to history.

THE PHANTOM FOWL OF POND SQUARE

Many of us treat ourselves to a bird as part of our Christmas celebrations. But did you know that the forerunner of many a frozen supermarket dinner once haunted a genteel part of London?

Pond Square in Highgate was plagued by something not usually encountered by your average ghost hunter – a phantom fowl!

In April 1626, Sir Francis Bacon found himself travelling through the snow-covered landscape of Highgate. John Aubrey in his *Brief Lives* described the events of that fateful spring day: 'As he was taking the air in a coach with Dr Witherborne (a Scotchman, physician to the King) towards Highgate, snow lay on the ground, and it came into my lord's thoughts why flesh might not be preserved in snow, as in salt. They were resolved they would try the experiment at once. They alighted out of the coach and went into a poor woman's house at the bottom of Highgate Hill, and bought a hen and made the woman gut it, and then stuffed the body with snow, and my lord did help to do it himself. The snow so chilled him, that he immediately fell so extremely ill that he could not return to his lodgings but went to the Earl of Arundel's house at Highgate, where they put him into a good bed warmed with a pan, but it was a damp bed that had not been laid in about a year before, which gave him such a cold that in two or three days, as I remember Mr Hobbes told me, he died of suffocation.'

You would expect Bacon to haunt the square, but I have yet to find a single account of his ghost making an appearance. However, there have been sightings of the creature involved in the fatal experiment.

POND SQUARE, HIGHGATE.

FRANCIS BACON
From a painting

The apparition of a chicken was seen many times over the years. It always appeared on winter nights, half running and half flying, near a brick wall in the square.

Mr. and Mrs. Greenhill lived in the square during the Second World War and often saw the animal. 'It was a big, whitish bird, and it used to perch on the lower boughs of the tree opposite our house,' said Mrs. Greenhill. 'Many members of my family have seen it on moonlit nights.'

In December 1943, aircraftman Terence Long was passing through the square when he heard the sounds of horses and the grind of wheels, followed by a shriek. He looked around and was amazed to see a squawking chicken with feathers missing, running around in circles, and shivering with cold. It then vanished.

A figure then appeared out of the darkness. It was an ARP firewatcher. 'Don't think I'm tipsy or anything,' said Long. 'But I've just seen a chicken that looked like a ghost. It had hardly any feathers, and it was dashing about as though it were freezing.'

The man did not appear surprised at hearing this and said, 'You've seen it, too, eh? You're not the first one. That fowl has been seen around these parts for years; for as long as I can remember.'

'Have you seen it?' Long asked.

The fire watcher shook his head and replied, 'No. But a month or two ago, some of the people round here saw a man actually trying to catch it. He chased it all round the square – probably thought it would help out his meat ration. It jumped and flew all over the place with this chap after it. THEN IT WENT STRAIGHT THROUGH A BRICK WALL!'

The bird was seen one January night in 1969 by a motorist who had broken down on a nearby street. He was walking through the square when he suddenly noticed a movement by a wall. He too saw a large white bird running around in circles and flapping its featherless wings. He assumed that the bird had been the victim of some heartless hooligan and angrily looked around for the culprit. Upon turning back, he found that the bird had disappeared. He then realised that the bird had made no sound despite appearing to be in great distress.

In February 1970, the ghost was seen again. A young couple saw what they described as a large white bird, almost devoid of feathers, fall to the ground as they were enjoying a cuddle. It flapped around a couple of times and then vanished into the darkness.

That was the last recorded sighting of the ghost of Pond Square, and I would imagine that the residents of Highgate are sincerely thankful for that. The last thing they need during the festive season is a phantom fowl disturbing their fun.

Chapter Thirteen

THE FIRST GHOST HUNTER: ELLIOTT O'DONNELL'S GHOSTLY CASEBOOK

Elliott O'Donnell was one of the foremost paranormal investigators of the 20th century. He was the first celebrity ghost hunter and appeared on BBC radio as early as the 1920s, where he thrilled listeners with tales of his ghostly adventures.

O'Donnell was born in Bristol in 1872 to an Irish father and an English mother. His family had its own banshee, which was heard to wail at the time of his father's mysterious death during a trip abroad; it was believed that he had been robbed and murdered by a travelling companion. O'Donnell also recalled, in the weeks following his death, a door being thrown open, the sounds of furniture being hurled around, disembodied footsteps going up the stairs, and, most terrifying of all, the sounds of his father jabbering incoherently.

O'Donnell's first sighting of a ghost was as a five-year-old, when he saw a naked elemental, some 6ft tall and covered in yellow spots, open the door and enter his bedroom. Its yellow-green eyes gazed at him intently for some minutes. O'Donnell felt no hostility from it, and the creature finally turned away and left the room.

In 1904, after a stint as an actor and a schoolmaster, he became a writer and spent the rest of his life studying psychic phenomena. Despite becoming a ghost hunter and conducting many night vigils on his own, O'Donnell never overcame the fear of being alone in the dark. This, however, did not prevent him from investigating many notoriously haunted locations across the UK. Over the next 60 years, he published over 50 books devoted to ghosts, true crime, and mysteries. He also wrote several novels. Such was his fame that O'Donnell was once described by P.G. Wodehouse as 'the Sherlock Holmes of the ghost world.' M.R. James also read his ghost stories and expressed the sincere hope that they were fiction, as life would be 'a risky business' if they were, in fact, true!

Some have criticised O'Donnell for failing to name witnesses and locations in many of his accounts. Several modern writers have even gone as far as to suggest that this was

Elliott O'Donnell.

because he made them up. However, many ghost hunters and authors of the time concealed names and locations at the request of the people involved. O'Donnell was also concerned about possible legal action and was fully aware of the pitfalls of naming a haunted location. 'As there have been several libel cases in connection with the alleged haunting of houses,' he commented, 'I have been obliged to give fictitious names to both people and localities.'

O'Donnell was also quite open about his abilities as a ghost hunter. He once said that he laid 'no claim to being what is termed a scientific psychical researcher. I am not a member of any August society that conducts its investigations of the other world, or worlds, with the test tube and weighing apparatus; neither do I pretend to be a medium or clairvoyant – I have never undertaken to "raise" ghosts at will for the sensation-seeker or the tourist.

'I am merely a ghost hunter. One who lays stake by his own eyes and senses; one who honestly believes he inherits in some degree the faculty of psychic perceptiveness from a long line of Celtic ancestry; and who is, and always has been, deeply and genuinely interested in all questions relative to phantasms and a continuance of individual life after physical dissolution.'

O'Donnell died in May 1965 after a long and varied career both as an author and paranormal investigator. Shortly before his death, he attended a meeting of the Ghost Club, where he spoke frankly to Peter Underwood about his lifelong interest in ghosts. 'Ghosts? I can't say I really know a great deal about them; perhaps I will know more when I become one, and then I'll try to contact you.' Sadly, as Underwood would later confirm, his friend never did.

O'Donnell's vast body of work continues to inspire and delight readers to this day. Indeed, many of his books are now happily back in print for a whole new generation to enjoy. Here is a selection of some of his most interesting cases.

THE 11 SKELETONS

Skellaw Wark lies in Cumbria. Around the year 1827, 11 male human skeletons were unearthed there. All had golden bangles on their wrists. It was thought that they were over 1,000 years old. The area in which they were found always had a reputation for being haunted, and the discovery of the skeletons appeared to increase the psychic activity there.

One lady told O'Donnell that she had seen 11 ghosts at Skellaw Wark. She was returning home with two of her sisters when they saw the tall, shadowy figure of a man emerge from some trees and cross the path in front of them. The figure was nude and glowed with a yellow-green light that appeared to emanate from within it. The figure walked to a large stone, where it stopped. The apparition raised its hand and shook it menacingly at them. It then sank into the ground. Another figure swiftly appeared, also of a similar appearance, and proceeded to repeat what the first figure had done. Eleven ghosts appeared in all.

The sisters fled home in terror and told their mother what they had witnessed. She explained that the figures were undoubtedly the ghosts of the men who had been dug up there. She then added that they were evil, as some misfortune always befell those who saw them. Sadly, her concerns quickly proved true. O'Donnell's informant separated from her fiancé, and her two sisters almost died after falling ill.

THE CLOCK

The year was 1909, and O'Donnell had made the acquaintance of a lady in Gloucester Place, London. She claimed that one night she had heard a clock on the landing outside her bedroom start to chime. There was nothing strange about that except for the fact that she had no clock on the landing! The lady counted 13 chimes in all. There was then a pause, and the clock chimed again some seven or so times. She asked if her husband had heard the clock, and he said yes.

Seven days later, her husband's friend died as a result of a skating accident. She told O'Donnell that her home was now plagued by strange sounds and asked him what she should do. He advised them to move as he felt that there was an evil presence in the house that resented the couple being there. The lady then confirmed that she felt it too and agreed to move out.

Portman Square W.

A few months went by, and O'Donnell found himself sitting next to the lady in a theatre. Despite her promise, she was still living in the house and mentioned that the previous night the clock had again chimed 13 and then chimed three. She was worried that it could mean that an unwell uncle was about to die. O'Donnell said maybe, but then suddenly got a strange feeling that her own death was being foretold by the clock. He decided to remain silent but did confide in his wife about this fear when he returned home. A few days later, he read of his friend's death in the *Daily Mail*. She had been killed in a traffic accident in Portman Square three days after hearing the clock chime. She had been sharing a taxi with a friend and a pet dog, but they remained unhurt in the crash. The driver also escaped unharmed. O'Donnell was convinced that the chimes were a warning, but had the evil presence, he wondered, also caused the accident to happen?

THE TREE

One evening, O'Donnell was out walking in Hyde Park when he came upon a tramp sitting on a bench. He decided to sit with him and, after remarking on the fair weather, offered the man some tobacco. The tramp did not reply, and O'Donnell repeated his offer. The man then answered, saying that it was food he needed as he had not eaten for two days. Fortunately, O'Donnell had a flask and sandwiches and offered them to him. After eating his fill, the man told O'Donnell about his life. He had been educated at a public school and had gone to Oxford. He then fell in with a bad lot, took to drinking, and was sent down. He went to the colonies but could not shake off his addiction to alcohol. This resulted in him losing job after job. He finally worked his way back to England, where he became a tramp.

O'Donnell then asked if he had ever experienced anything supernatural. The man then told him of something strange that had happened to him in the park in which they now sat: 'I was wandering about the park one night, looking for some spot where I could lie down without being seen by any of the keepers or police. For some time I met with no success, but at last I espied a tree, away from the path and occupying a very isolated position. It was a singular-looking tree, inasmuch as it had, growing almost horizontally from its trunk, one long branch that strikingly resembled a very long human arm, with a hand outstretched and all the fingers widespread and curled, as if in the act of clutching hold of someone. Still, as its foliage was thick and there was a depression or hollow in the ground exactly beneath it, I fancied it was just the place I was in search of. When one has no night clothes of any description, no sheets, and no blankets, it does not take long to get into bed, and in a few seconds, I was lying in the hollow, with my coat and trousers pulled tightly around me, trying to imagine myself warm. Fortunately, the night was not very cold, and, being very tired, I was soon asleep, and, for a wonder, sound asleep.

'At first, all was blank, and then suddenly I dreamed. I fancied the long, grotesquely fashioned, horizontal branch immediately above me turned into an actual living arm and

Hyde Park

hand, and began slowly to descend, the fingers all widespread, ready to grip hold of me. I was at once seized with an awful horror, but found myself, as one often does in dreams, utterly unable to do anything. I couldn't move a limb or even a muscle.

'In this hopeless condition, I was forced to watch the arm descend lower and lower, until the great hand hovered just above my face and the tips of the long and cruel-looking fingers all but grazed my flesh. A voice then said, in soft but decidedly menacing tones, "I have got you now, and I mean to keep you, always, always, always – there is no escape."

'The next moment the fingers, soft as satin, closed over my mouth and throat and began to throttle me. I awoke shrieking and in such terror that I jumped up and sought a bed elsewhere.'

The tramp then explained to O'Donnell that he could not get the dream out of his head. He was fascinated by it and decided to sleep under the tree again. When he did, he had exactly the same dream. He had intended to sleep there a third time, but a man he knew stopped him with a warning not to do so as it was an unlucky place. The man went on to explain that several people had killed themselves at the spot after spending a night beneath the tree.

The tramp then told O'Donnell that he believed something vampirish formed under the tree at night, something that hated human beings and wanted to destroy them.

O'Donnell asked to see the tree, which he found standing alone in the middle of a wide-open space. He decided to stand under it despite the protests of the tramp. He asked for the man's name and discovered that he was called George Howell. O'Donnell gave him a couple of shillings and told him to get a decent night's sleep. Howell thanked him and said that if he needed him in the future, he could find him on the bench where they had first met.

O'Donnell was now alone. He leaned against the tree and waited. The minutes ticked by, and as it turned 1am, he started to think of going home. He then suddenly began to feel as if he was not alone. It became so unbearable that he hurriedly left the park.

A few months went by, and O'Donnell saw George again. He was sitting on the same bench. This time he had a woman sitting close to him. O'Donnell asked George if he had been tempted to sleep under the tree again.

George explained that he had been but had fought the urge. He also said that a man had been found dead under it a couple of nights ago. The woman, whose name was Minnie, confirmed the tree's evil reputation and said that a friend of hers had slept under it and had been seized with fearful dreams about being strangled.

O'Donnell left the pair and did not see them for several weeks. One day, he returned to the park and saw Minnie sitting alone on the bench. She recognised him and said that George was dead. She explained that he had died a few days after their last meeting. George had become obsessed with the tree and would not stop talking about it. He insisted on sleeping under it again and found himself experiencing exactly the same dream as before. Despite her protests, he then went back there the very next night. He was found dead in the morning, strangled by his braces. It was assumed to be suicide. The tree was later cut down.

THE CHELSEA HORROR

A clergyman was looking for a place to rent and found himself in Chelsea being shown around a house by a lad from an estate agent. He was alone on the first floor when he heard a sound like the click of a door handle. He turned around and saw a door begin to open. It had only opened a few inches when a hand suddenly appeared. It was clearly a woman's hand, as the fingers were long and tapering. The nails were polished and almond-shaped. The clergyman was fascinated by the delicate hand and found that he could not take his eyes from it. The smell of perfume suddenly filled the air, and the hand pulled back and the door closed.

He assumed that someone else was looking over the house and thought nothing more of it. He returned downstairs to the hall, where he mentioned to the boy that a lady was upstairs. The lad appeared alarmed and explained that the owner was a widower and lived alone. No one else was viewing the house that day. The clergyman suggested the boy go and look for himself. They then went upstairs together and arrived at the door in question. All was still, and they entered the room. It was empty. There was no other exit, and it would have been impossible for the lady to have left the house unseen.

That night, the man could not stop thinking about the woman's hand. He even found himself dreaming about the experience as he slept. He decided to take the house, and within a week he was living there with his wife and children.

A few days after moving in, his wife told him that Mary, their maid, was drunk. She had seen Mary in the kitchen, stinking of drink, giggling, and talking nonsense. The clergyman expressed surprise, as she had previously been of good character. His wife explained that she had given her notice and then asked if he thought there was anything strange about the house. She then went on to explain that she felt as if she was constantly being watched. She had also been in the bedroom, making the bed, when she heard someone knock at the door. She called out for them to come in and then heard the door open and someone cross the floor. She turned around and found herself alone. Was the place haunted, she wondered?

Her husband scoffed at such a notion but could not help thinking of his experience on his first visit to the property. A couple of days passed, and he found himself alone in the house after returning from a service. He was sitting in a chair when he heard the sounds of high heels climbing the stairs from the basement. The footsteps then entered the hall, and the smell of perfume filled the air. The clergyman recognised it as the scent that he had smelt on his first visit to the house. He felt strangely intoxicated by it but could see no one. The footsteps continued towards him, and cold, soft fingers touched his forehead lightly. The folds of a garment appeared to brush over his feet as the unseen figure then made for the front door, which opened and then closed. The room became icy cold, and the man found himself shivering uncontrollably. A wild desire then took hold of him, and he rushed out in pursuit of the unseen female. The street was deserted. He ran on, convinced that he would find her, until fatigue forced him to take a rest in a public house.

He had never been interested in alcohol, but the atmosphere inside strangely appealed to him, and he began drinking. After an hour or so, he arrived home drunk and found his shocked wife waiting for him. She fled upstairs in tears and sought solace in sleep. She was woken by the clock striking two. She then heard her door open and someone enter the room. She saw a woman's hand. The fingers were long and tapering, with the nails beautifully shaped and polished. She could see nothing beyond the wrist as the hand moved towards her. Its fingers then rested on her forehead.

The hand withdrew, and she heard footsteps retreating to the door, which opened and then closed. She was not frightened in the least by this and began to think of how disgusted she was with her husband. She could not believe that he had come home stinking of whisky. He was nothing more than a beast! She decided that she could never forgive him and made the decision to leave him and return to her parents. She got dressed, packed her bags, and left as it became daylight.

The clergyman could not believe that he had been deserted by his wife. He felt crushed and betrayed, but then began to think of the scented hand and began to revel at the thought of seeing it again. His two children, John and Emma, appeared to be unconcerned by the departure of their mother despite having been previously devoted to her. They began to act

The Pig-Faced Lady.

out of character, quarrelling with their governess and generally causing mischief. Emma suddenly took delight in torturing flies. She once even caught a mouse in a trap and, joined by her brother, tortured it to death.

It is hardly surprising to learn that the governess quit her position in disgust, leaving the children to do as they pleased. They slept in the nursery, and Emma was awakened not long after the departure of the governess by someone moving about in the room. She thought it was her brother and called on him to be quiet. He did not respond, and so she sat up and looked. She saw a tall figure, illuminated by moonlight, standing in the centre of the room. It was covered in a black cloak. It then glided towards the door, beckoning Emma to follow it. The girl noticed two lovely white hands, clearly those of a female. She awakened John, and the two followed the woman out of the room.

The figure crossed the landing, descended two flights of stairs, and stopped outside their father's door. It then threw aside its cloak to reveal a hideous sight. The body was that of a beautiful woman, but the head, crowned by lovely golden hair, was that of a monster. The cheeks were of white, unwholesome fat, and the nose was like a pig's snout. To make matters worse, the mouth was a slit and the teeth were great, deformed tusks. Suddenly, their father opened the door, and the fearful apparition faded away.

The clergyman and his children fled the house the following day. O'Donnell wrote that the children's characters soon returned to normal and that the father and mother were soon reconciled. The house had a succession of tenants in the following years, and O'Donnell was told that it continued to be badly haunted. He believed the apparition could be a Vice Elemental, a creature that possibly lingered there because of some foul deed committed on the site long ago. He further speculated that the pig-faced woman could even be the earthbound spirit of a woman who had once lived there but could not leave due to her base, earthly desires and passions. Was it possible that her degenerate nature had affected the clergyman and his family? If so, it was fortunate that they escaped its evil influence.

Chapter Fourteen

MORE TALES FROM ELLIOTT O'DONNELL'S GHOSTLY CASEBOOK

THE LITTLE GIRL

O'Donnell heard of a strange haunting in St. Helen's Church in Worcester. A woman told him that her mother had been viewing the church one late afternoon when she saw a young girl, in deep mourning, frantically searching for something on the floor of one of the aisles. The girl then raised her head and looked at her. She was crying and appeared ill. The lady spoke to her and asked what she had lost, offering to help her find it.

SOUTH END OF HIGH STREET, WITH ST. HELEN'S CHURCH.

The interior of St Helen's Church, Worcester.

The child did not reply and ran into the chancel, where she vanished. An uncanny feeling came over the lady, and she left the church. Despite this, she returned the next day and again saw the girl running into the chancel after searching for something on the floor.

Encountering an official of the church, she asked about the girl. The man seemed scared and tried to evade the question. He then admitted that the apparition had been seen several times by visitors. Who she was, what she was looking for, and why she haunted the church were questions that he was unable to answer.

THE SCYTHE

St. Mary's churchyard in Barnard Castle, County Durham, has a figure of Death, holding a scythe, on the tomb of George Hopper, who died in 1725. A certain Mrs. Hunt once told O'Donnell a curious story connected with the figure. Her grandfather, an army officer, lived near Barnard Castle. He was on leave one day when he suddenly saw a raven fly by him. He followed it with his eyes and then noticed the figure of death on the tomb. As he did so, he saw the scythe move. Assuming he was seeing things, he rubbed his eyes and looked again. The scythe was still moving, and the figure itself seemed to be gazing at him intently. One of his friends asked what he was looking at, and the moment he spoke, the scythe stopped moving. The next day, the officer's father died.

Several weeks passed, and the man mentioned the incident to an old inhabitant of the town. She said that there was a tradition connected with the church. If a raven was seen to fly from the figure of Death and the scythe moved, it would mean the death of the person who witnessed it or someone close to them.

The figure of death, St Mary's Churchyard.

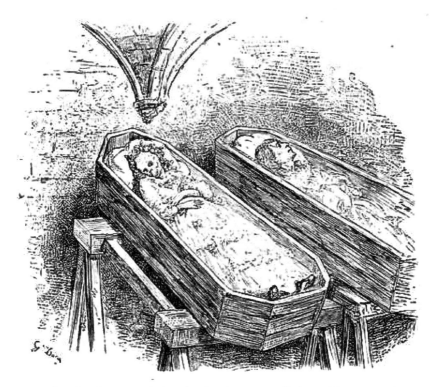

A burial vault in a Lincolnshire churchyard was supposedly haunted by an angry ghost.

THE COFFINS

O'Donnell once heard of an unnamed church in Lincolnshire that was witness to a strange event in the 18th century. The local squire lost his wife and child within a year, and their bodies were laid to rest in the family vault beneath the church. The squire had not spoken to his younger brother for several years due to the latter's having had a bitter feud with the squire's wife.

The parson decided to bring about a reconciliation between the two, and the estranged brother was invited to live at the hall on the condition that he never mention the name of his deceased sister-in-law.

A year went by, and relations between the brothers had greatly improved when an epidemic broke out in the village. The brother of the squire was one of the victims, and as he lay dying, he was urged by the parson to repent of his sins and forgive all those who he believed had injured him over the years. He then mentioned the squire's wife. The dying brother became very angry and, using the last of his strength, exclaimed, 'I know that I am dying, but mark my words: if, when I am dead, you dare to bury me in the same vault with that accused woman, the living, as well as the dead, shall hear of me.'

He then fell back and died. The parson decided not to inform the squire of what had passed, and his brother's body was placed in the family vault alongside those of his wife and daughter.

That same night, terrible groans and shrieks were heard coming from the vault. The parson then decided to inform the squire of his brother's threats, and it was decided to open the vault. Upon entering it, they were met with a shocking sight. The coffins of the squire's wife and daughter were lying at the far end of the vault. The daughter's coffin was lying across her mother's, as if to protect it. Close to them was the brother's coffin, standing erect.

The vault was thoroughly examined, and there were no signs of its being opened since the interment of the squire's brother. The coffins were restored to their original places, and the vault was once again sealed. That night, the frightful sounds were heard again by those keeping watch outside. News soon spread of the strange events at the church, and it was suggested that an explosion of foul air, caused by the rotting bodies, had caused the coffins to move.

The squire decided to have ventilators added to the vault, but this made no difference as the sounds continued. Finally, he decided to construct a strong brick wall between the coffins of his wife and brother. From that moment on, the vault remained silent.

THE GARGOYLE

A certain Mr. Baker once told O'Donnell of a gargoyle in a Sussex church. He was looking around the building when he saw its face slowly change into the image of one of his maiden aunts, who was very close to him. It then changed back into the gargoyle. The same evening, he received a telegram informing him that his aunt was dead. She had died at the same time that her face appeared on the stone image.

A few days later, he mentioned the incident to the vicar of the church. The vicar confided in him that he was not the first to see the gargoyle change. The year before, a female member of the congregation had been arranging flowers for the Harvest Thanksgiving when she heard a malevolent chuckle. She turned around and was drawn to the gargoyle. As she stared at it, it changed into an urn draped in black. To make sure she was not hallucinating, the woman pressed one eye. If it was a hallucination, it would remain the same; if she was really seeing it, it would appear double. The urn appeared double. What she was seeing was real. The following day, one of her closest relatives died.

The vicar told the man that he was convinced the gargoyle was a harbinger of death and hoped its transformation would never take place during a service. 'Imagine what a commotion that would make!' he exclaimed.

THE BOOK

Another of O'Donnell's informants, whom he chose to call Mrs. Bright, wrote to him about a church in Bournemouth. She declined to give its name, as she had promised the vicar not to reveal its location to another soul. She had been walking by the church one

Elliott O'Donnell was one of the foremost ghost hunters of the 20th century.

day when she saw a tall, well-dressed lady in grey beckon to her by name. She crossed the road and asked what she wanted. The lady would have been attractive but for her teeth, which stuck out. Her eyes were also too close together, and her general appearance struck Mrs. Bright as not being pleasant. The woman was clearly intelligent and spoke in cultivated tones, but it was hard to place her accent. It was not Irish or Scottish, and yet it did not appear foreign. She then asked Mrs. Bright to do her a favour. She explained that three years ago, the vicar of the church had lent her a book. It was a prize that he had won at a public school. 'I went abroad soon after. The vicar has written to me several times about it, as he values it greatly and wants it back, but I haven't been able to answer his letters. Will you be very kind and tell him that Mrs. King has it? It is put away with a number of other books in a kind of lumber room.'

Mrs. Bright asked why she could not tell him herself as she was a stranger to the area. She also asked how she knew her name. 'We'll call it telepathy,' she replied. 'Let that suffice. Reasons which I can't explain to you prevent me from telling the vicar in person. Please do me this favour.'

Mrs. Bright reluctantly agreed and asked for her name. 'Mrs. Gibbons,' she replied, ''Dora Gibbons; and now I must hurry off, for I have a very long way to go, and time is pressing.'

Mrs. Gibbons then thanked her, smiled, and quickly walked away. That same evening, Mrs. Bright saw the vicar of the church and delivered the message. The vicar looked very grave and asked for a description of Mrs. Gibbons. The description matched that of a Mrs. Gibbons who was known to the vicar. She had died abroad some 12 months earlier.

The vicar contacted Mrs. King and asked about the book. It was found in the exact place described by the ghost.

THE WATCH

A friend of O'Donnell's who had served in the South African Wars was visiting Clifton in Bristol and decided to attend a service in St. Mary's, Redcliffe. He arrived early and decided to sit at the back of the church in case he had to leave early. Shortly afterwards, a girl of about 11 years of age walked noiselessly up the aisle and sat down a few rows in front of him. She was wearing a felt hat with a school ribbon and a dark blue coat and shirt. She looked familiar to him, and when she turned around, he saw it was his goddaughter, Delphine Kent, who was the daughter of an old school friend of his. She smiled at him and pointed to a gold watch on her wrist.

He nodded to her and then thought of an incident that had occurred just before he left for South Africa. He had given Delphine a gold wristlet watch and had become very

St Mary Redcliffe, Bristol.

149

angry with her after she had lost it while playing with her friends in the garden. She took his anger badly and refused to kiss him when he left. She also said that she hoped she would never see him again.

Delphine continued to smile at him in the church, but was soon lost to view as the rows between them filled with people. He wondered why she was alone and, during the first hymn, looked towards her seat. She had gone. He occupied a seat next to the aisle, and it would have been impossible for her to leave the church without being seen. He suddenly had a foreboding of ill and decided to leave the church. The next day, he sought out Delphine's parents. Both looked dejected.

'Where's Delphine?' he asked. 'I saw her in church last night.'

'You must have been mistaken. Delphine's dead,' Mr. Kent said. He then explained that she had died six months earlier of pneumonia.

Mr. Kent then asked how Delphine was dressed, and it emerged that the clothes she had been wearing in the church matched exactly her school uniform. Her father also mentioned the incident with the watch. It had been found in the hollow of a tree. Delphine must have placed it there for safety. He then explained that she had wanted very much to write to her godfather to say it had been found. Sadly, she did not know his address. Almost her last words on her deathbed were for him: 'Be sure to give him my love.'

'I have no doubt whatever it was her spirit you saw in church,' her father said. 'She was permitted to come back to tell you about the watch. She was so terribly upset at losing it.'

THE HOUSE OF DEATH

An ordinary-looking house in Croydon had a very sinister reputation in the early years of the 20th century. Tenant after tenant died in the house or left it in some haste. Rumours began to circulate that it was haunted, and people would hurry past it at night in fear of what they might see. Such was its reputation that it was left empty for years. The house came to the attention of the press, and a reporter decided to spend the night there to see what would happen. The man found that some items of furniture had been left in the house, and he settled himself into an old armchair in a room on the ground floor. Just after midnight, a feeling of sickness overcame him, and he became aware of something loathsome entering the room through the closed door. He sensed it getting closer and closer until it finally enveloped where he sat. He fainted, and when he recovered, the presence had gone. He left the house in some haste, but the shock of what had happened affected him badly, and, despite having previously been in sound health, he died within two weeks. O'Donnell later learned that the house had been demolished. No reason was ever found for the haunting.

Elliott O'Donnell.

THE SEVERED ARM

A man was visiting Perth in Scotland for a week. On the night of his arrival, he went to bed early and was soon fast asleep. He was suddenly awoken with a start and found himself staring up at the ceiling. The room was filled with moonlight, and one of his hands was hanging over the bed. He was suddenly gripped by an icy hand that was missing a middle finger, the shock of which caused him to almost faint. Despite this, he grabbed the hand and found that the arm terminated at the elbow. This time the shock proved too great, and he passed out. When he came around, the arm had vanished.

At breakfast, he told his host what had happened. The man appeared shocked and begged him to say no more. He said that an ancestor of his had killed himself in the room where his guest had slept. He had lost a middle finger on one of his hands and now haunted the room intermittently. If the arm grabbed hold of you, it was believed that some terrible misfortune would soon occur. As he finished speaking, a maid came into the room and handed him a telegram. It informed him that his youngest son had died suddenly.

Chapter Fifteen

THE HORRORS OF GLAMIS

Glamis Castle in Scotland is the ancestral home of the Earls of Strathmore, who have lived there since the 14th century.

It is said to be Scotland's most haunted castle, with numerous tales of ghostly happenings taking place within its dark and forbidding walls. A young Walter Scott went to Glamis in 1790 and noted the castle's oppressive atmosphere. He would later write, 'I must own, as I heard door after door shut … I began to consider myself as too far from the living and somewhat too near to the dead.'

THE LIVING TOMB

One of the most horrific stories concerns the Ogilvie family. They were at war with the Lindsays, and one day they unwisely sought refuge from Lord Glamis. He agreed and hid them in a room at the castle. Little did the Ogilvies realise that Lord Glamis hated them too – he locked the door and left them to starve to death.

GLAMIS CASTLE.   201423

Centuries later, one of the Earls of Strathmore came across the room and had it opened. He found the skeletons of the Ogilvies. It was clear from the state of the remains that they had gnawed the flesh from their arms as they slowly died of hunger. The sight was so terrifying that he ordered the room bricked up forever. The ghosts of the Ogilvies are said to linger still, hammering on the walls.

Andrew Green, the author of several books on ghosts, was told by a Mrs. Hunter that she had often heard loud crashes coming from the oldest part of the castle. These sounds were always heard at 4am. Were these noises a re-enactment of the Ogilvies' last desperate attempts to escape their living tomb?

THE TONGUELESS WOMAN

Another legend concerns a guest who was once strolling in the castle grounds at midnight when he looked up and saw a distressed-looking woman staring out from a tower window. She suddenly screamed and disappeared as if someone had pulled her away from the window. A few minutes later, an old woman was seen emerging from a door at the base of the tower. She was carrying a sack and quickly vanished into the nearby woods.

Years later, the man was in Italy when he was caught in a snowstorm. He sought shelter in a monastery, where the monks told him about a British woman who was kept in a nearby nunnery. Her tongue had been cut out and her hands cut off after she discovered a terrible family secret in a house where she had been a servant. He asked to see the woman and recognised her as the face he had seen at Glamis.

In death, the unfortunate woman returned to Glamis. Her ghost now runs across the castle lawns, pointing to her bloody mouth.

THE DEVIL AND EARL BEARDIE

His Satanic Majesty is said to have once visited Glamis. Alexander Lindsay, the fourth Earl of Crawford, who was known as Earl Beardie, was playing cards one Saturday night at Glamis when a servant reminded him that he should stop as it was almost the Sabbath. Beardie dismissed him, saying that he would carry on and even play with the Devil himself if the fancy took him. These words were hardly out of Beardie's mouth when a stranger suddenly appeared and offered to join in his game. The man then asked for Beardie to sign a bond for whatever he desired if the Earl lost. Beardie rashly agreed, and the two men began their game, with the Earl shouting and cursing as the night dragged on. One servant, curious to see what was happening in the room, put his eye to the keyhole. The stranger noticed this and shouted, 'Smite that eye!' whereupon the servant was blinded by a dart of flame. With this, the man vanished. It was only then that Beardie realised that he had been playing with the Devil himself!

According to the legend, Beardie had signed away his soul and, upon his death, was cursed to play cards until the day of judgement. The sounds of his swearing are still said

to be heard from time to time, and his tall, bearded ghost has been seen in various parts of the castle. One sighting occurred in 1871 when Mrs. Wingfield, the daughter of Lord Castletown, awoke one night in the Blue Room and saw what she described as 'a huge old man with a long flowing beard' seated in front of the fire. His face was that of a corpse.

In the 1950s, a cook, Florence Foster, claimed to have heard rattling dice, swearing, and stamping late at night. She had also heard someone knock three times on her bedroom door, but no one was there when she opened it. She would lie awake in bed shaking with fright and finally decided to resign from her job rather than hear the sounds again.

A woman and her son once stayed in the castle. One night, the mother was disturbed by a blast of cold air, which extinguished her night light. She saw a tall figure in armour leave her room and head into the dressing room where her son was sleeping. The child awoke with a cry and told his mother that 'a giant' had stood over his bed and stared at him.

THE WHITE LADY

The White Lady is thought to be the ghost of Janet Douglas, the wife of John, the sixth Lord Glamis. She was the sister of George Douglas, the Earl of Angus, who had married the widowed Queen Margaret after the Battle of Flodden. Her brother gained control over the young King James V, and such was his strictness that James came to hate the Douglas clan.

Janet's husband died in 1528, and she remarried in 1532. Her new husband was Archibald Campbell of Skipness. Allegations were soon made that she had poisoned her first husband and conspired with the Douglas clan against the King. As a result of this,

Crypt, Glamis Castle

Janet, her 16-year-old son John, and her husband were imprisoned in Edinburgh Castle. Campbell tried to escape but fell to his death on the rocks below the castle walls. Janet's servants were tortured to extract false evidence against her, and in 1537, almost blind after her long incarceration, she was burned at the stake outside the castle.

Her son John had also been found guilty and was sentenced to death. However, because of his youth, he was spared and kept in Edinburgh Castle. The Glamis estate was then seized by the king. John was finally released after the death of James and had Glamis restored to him by an act of the Scottish Parliament. Due to the terrible nature of her death, Janet was unable to find peace in the afterlife, and her ghost was said to have returned to Glamis, where she was seen floating above the clock tower, surrounded by the lurid glow of a fire.

THE BARREL

One of the strangest hauntings connected with the castle concerns a barrel at the top of a flight of stairs. It was said to tip over by itself and chase the maids down the steps, especially on their first day at Glamis. When they looked back, the barrel was back at the top of the stairs. Clearly a ghost with a sense of humour!

THE MOANING WOMAN

Violet Tweedale, in her book *Ghosts I Have Seen* (1919), wrote of a Lady Reay who once stayed at the castle: 'On the fourth night I was awakened by a moaning sound in my room, and I opened my eyes. The room was in total darkness, but I saw something very bright near the door. I shut my eyes instantly and pulled the bedclothes over my head in a

GLAMMIS CASTLE,
FORFARSHIRE

paroxysm of fear. I longed to light my candles but didn't dare, and the moaning continued, and I thought I should go quite mad.

'At last, I ventured to peep out again. I saw a woman dressed exactly like Mary Tudor in her pictures, and she was wandering round the walls, flinging herself against them like a bird against the bars of a cage, and beating her hands upon the walls, and all the time she moaned horribly. I'm sure she was the ghost of a mad woman. Her face and form were lit up exactly like a picture thrown upon a magic lantern screen, and every detail of her dress was clearly defined.

'Luckily, she never looked at me, or I should have screamed, and I thought of Lord and Lady I. sleeping in the next room to mine and wondered how I could reach them. I was really too terrified to move, and the ghost kept more or less to that part of the room where the door was situated.

'I must have lain there awake for two or three hours, sometimes with my head buried under the clothes, sometimes peeping out, when at last the moaning suddenly stopped. I opened my eyes. Thank God, I was alone. The ghost had departed.'

THE STORM

Violet Tweedale knew Captain Eric Streatfield of the Gordon Highlanders, who was a nephew of Lord Strathmore. He also saw the Tudor lady, but later had an even stranger experience at Glamis. In her book, she recorded what happened: 'Whilst, as a schoolboy, he was visiting Glamis Castle with his parents, he noticed that they began to behave in rather a peculiar manner. They were often consulting alone with one another and constantly scanning the sky from their bedroom window, which adjoined his. For two or three days this sort of thing went on, and he caught queer fragments of conversation whispered between them, such as, "It doesn't always happen. We might be spared this year, but the power must die out someday." At last, one evening, his father called him into his room, where his mother stood by the open window. In his hand, his father held an open watch. His mother bade him look out and tell them what sort of night it was. He replied that it was fine and still and cold, and the stars were beginning to appear.

'His father then said, "We want you to take particular note of the weather, for in another moment you may witness a remarkable change. Probably you will see a furious tempest." Eric could not make head or tail of this. He wondered if his parents had gone mad, but glancing at his mother, he noticed that she looked strangely pale and anxious. Then the storm burst with such terrific suddenness and fury that it terrified him. A howling tempest, accompanied by blinding lightning and deafening thunder, rushed down upon them from an absolutely clear sky. His mother knelt down by the bed, and he thought that she was praying. When Eric asked for an explanation, he was told that when he was grown up, one would be given to him. Unfortunately, the moment never came.'

THE GREY LADY

A mysterious Grey Lady haunts the 17th-century chapel. Lady Granville told the author James Wentworth Day that she was sitting in the chapel one sunny afternoon playing music when she got the feeling that someone was behind her. She looked back and saw the Grey Lady praying. 'I distinctly saw the detail of her dress and the outline of her figure,' she said, 'but the sun, shining through the windows, shone through her and made a pattern on the floor.' The ghost was also seen by Earl Strathmore. He was looking at some pictures in the chapel when he saw a figure in grey kneeling in one of the pews. Not wishing to disturb her, he politely tiptoed away.

James Wentworth Day was told that Glamis Chapel was haunted by a Grey Lady.

The Grey Lady,

THE MONSTER OF GLAMIS

The most famous legend of Glamis concerns a hidden room and the 'monster.' Charles George Harper wrote of it in his 1907 book *Haunted Houses*: 'There are, in fact, several "secret" chambers in the ancient 15ft-thick walls, but these are neither more nor less a matter of secrecy than the so-called "secret" drawers that form so perfectly obvious a feature of most old escritoires. The one absolutely secret chamber is never known to more than three persons at one time: to the Earl of Strathmore for the time being, to his eldest son (or to the next heir), and to the factor, or steward, of the estate. The solemn initiation ceremony takes place upon the coming of age of the heir, on the night of his 21st birthday, when the three are supposed to be armed with crowbars to break down the masonry which walls up the mystic recess. This rite duly performed and the wall again built up, the factor invariably leaves the castle and rides for home, no matter how stormy the night or late the hour. The Lyon family is wealthy – the late Earl left over a million sterling – and could easily reside elsewhere, but on the night that witnesses the coming of age of the heir, its members will be all gathered together at Glamis.'

Claude Bowes-Lyon, the 13th Earl, once told a friend, 'If you could guess the nature of this secret, you would go down on your knees and thank God it was not yours.' He was also said to have paid for a workman and his family to emigrate to Australia after he accidentally came across a passageway leading to the secret room.

Augustus Hare visited the castle in October 1877 and spoke of the Earl's 'ever-sad look.' He recalled the event in his multi-volume autobiography, *The Story of My Life*: The Bishop of Brechin, who was a great friend of the house, felt this strange sadness so deeply that he went to Lord Strathmore and said how, having heard of this strange secret which oppressed him, he could not help entreating him to make use of his services as an ecclesiastic. … Lord Strathmore was deeply moved. He said he thanked him, but that in his most unfortunate position, no one could ever help him.'

Andrew Ralston was a servant at the castle in the last decades of the 19th century. He had been initiated into the mystery and was so upset by the experience that he vowed never again to spend a night in the castle. On one occasion, after a heavy fall of snow, he is said to have refused an invitation to stay overnight at Glamis and instead roused the servants and had them clear a path to his house, which lay more than a mile away.

Ralston once discussed Glamis's secret with Frances, Countess of Strathmore, who was the 13th Earl's wife and grandmother of Queen Elizabeth, the Queen Mother. The Countess asked Ralston to reveal the secret to her, but he refused, saying, 'It is fortunate that you do not know it and can never know it, for if you did know, you would not be a happy woman.'

In the 19th century, a party was held at the castle during the absence of the Earl, and the guests, headed by the Countess, sought to find the hidden room. They started to hang towels from all the windows but were thwarted by the unexpected return of Strathmore, who soon put a stop to their investigation.

The *New York Sun* wrote of the hidden room in 1904, 'On one occasion, a young doctor who was staying in the castle professionally found on returning to his bedroom that the carpet had been taken up and relayed. He noted that the mark of the carpet was different at one end of the room. By moving the furniture and raising the carpet, he laid bare a trap door, which he forced open and found himself in a passage. This passage ended in a cement wall. The cement was still soft, leaving the impression of a finger. He returned to his room – and next morning received a cheque for his services with the intimation that the carriage was ready to take him to the station for the first train.'

The secret of the hidden chamber died with Claude Bowes-Lyon in 1904, his heir having flatly refused to be told the secret on coming of age.

So what was the terrible secret? It is alleged that in 1821, a male heir, the first son of Thomas, Lord Glamis, was born terribly deformed. The boy supposedly died soon after his birth, but rumours began to circulate that he was still alive and had been hidden in a secret room. He supposedly lived on for decades and did not die until 1921. The Mad Earl's Walk on the roof of the castle is said to be where the poor soul was exercised.

A variation of this tale is to be found in a diary entry from *Notes from the Life of an Ordinary Mortal* by A.G.C. Liddell (London, 1911), 'Aug. 21. A foreign lady here is lively and amusing. She pretends to a belief that she has lived several previous lives, which enabled her to make astonishing statements as to what she has done and whom she had met in her former existence, e.g., it comes with great effect into a conversation on astronomy to say, "As Galileo once told me."

'Spiritualism is another of her topics. Being herself a wonderful medium, male spirits were always falling in love with her. At one time she was persecuted by an aged spirit who showed his attentions by knocking about the furniture of her boudoir and who, at last, became so importunate as actually to rock the chair on which she sat. She could only get rid of him by directing the governess to make overtures to him; when he desisted from his attentions, with what result to the governess she did not say.

'Among her other marvels was the best account of the Glamis ghost which I have yet heard. As she was sitting in her room there the wall became transparent, and she saw through it into the secret chamber illumined with a lurid light. There lay in chains a fearful object, half man, half toad, who was Lord Strathmore in 1330. The dash of the toad in his structure had given him longevity; the amount of man in him was such that they dare not knock him on the head, so there he remains, fed on raw flesh by Lord Strathmore, the factor and the eldest son.'

Yet another version of the secret claims that a female servant of Glamis was found to be a vampire. She was walled up in the room and remains there, waiting for release and the chance to find new victims to satisfy her terrible blood lust.

Chapter Sixteen

THE WOMAN IN BLACK:
THE DESPARDS

St. Anne's House, on the corner of Pittville Circus Road and All Saints Road in Cheltenham, Gloucestershire, was haunted by a ghost that was witnessed or heard by some 20 people over a period of four years. The matter was investigated by Frederic W.H. Myers on behalf of the Society for Psychical Research, and his account of the case was published in the society's journal in 1892 under the title 'Record of a Haunted House' (earlier references to the haunting had been made by Eleanor Sidgwick in an 1885 edition of the journal). Myers had been told about the ghost by Mr. J.W. Graham, the principal of Dalton Hall, Manchester, who, in turn, had been told about it by Captain Despard, who lived in the house with his family. However, in this report, Myers did not reveal the location of the house and protected the identity of the family by calling them the

Did a ghostly woman dressed in black once haunt this Cheltenham house?

Mortons. The name of the family was not revealed until the 1940s, when a book devoted to the case was published.

The haunting has been cited as one of the most impressive in the history of the paranormal, although later investigators such as Peter Underwood have cast doubt on the case, suggesting a more earthly explanation.

The detached three-storey house, with 14 rooms, was built in the early 1860s and occupied the site of a former market garden. The first owners were Henry and Elisabeth Swinhoe, who moved there in 1865. The couple lived there happily, but in August 1866 Elizabeth died in childbirth. She was only 35. Mr. Swinhoe, grief-stricken, took to drinking, but in February 1870 he married again. His new wife, Imogen, hoped to cure him of his alcoholism but soon succumbed to drinking herself. However, Henry Swinhoe's granddaughter, Violet Rhodes James, told Andrew MacKenzie, a later investigator of the case, that Imogen had a drinking problem prior to the marriage and was actually the one responsible for her husband's addiction to alcohol. Whatever the case, the new marriage was far from happy, and the couple often had heated arguments that sometimes led to violence. Henry later claimed that his wife had thrown furniture at him and used indecent language. Some of the rows concerned the care of his five children and the possession of the first Mrs. Swinhoe's jewellery, which Henry decided to hide under the floorboards in the morning room. According to Mrs. James, the children from the first marriage suffered 'years of tyranny and misery under Imogen'.

The marriage broke down irretrievably in 1875, with Mrs. Swinhoe moving out. Mr. Swinhoe started divorce proceedings and even had a statement published in the Cheltenham Mercury stating that he would not be responsible for any of his wife's debts. The couple divorced in May of the same year.

Henry Swinhoe died at the house, then known as 'Garden Reach,' in July 1876. His ex-wife died in Clifton on September 23, 1878, from alcoholism, aged 41. Her body was taken to Cheltenham, and she was buried alongside her parents in a vault beneath Holy Trinity. A memorial plaque to her is still on view inside the church.

The house was purchased by Benjamin Littlewood and his wife in 1879. They were not destined to enjoy it for long. Benjamin died within a month of moving in – in the same room as Mr. Swinhoe – and his widow decided to leave the property.

In 1880, Garden Reach was bought by a man who changed its name to Pittville Hall. He stayed there for only a few months before moving out.

By this time, the house was said to be haunted by a woman in black, but its new owner always denied experiencing anything unusual during his time there. However, it is interesting to note that the house was in a fashionable part of Cheltenham, yet the rent was now only £60, half of what it should have been. Also, between 1860 and 1913, the house was empty for nine years at varying periods. None of the other houses in the

I, HENRY SWINHOE, of Garden Reach, Pittville, Chelltenham, will Not be Responsible for any Debt or Debts that Mrs IMOGEN or HENRY SWINHOE may contract in her or my name, nor will I pay any Debt or Debts that may have been contracted by MRS SWINHOE, and for which I am not legally responsible.
Garden Reach, Cheltenham ;
25th March, 1875.

street were ever empty for so long. This would suggest that the building was getting a bad reputation and was proving difficult to rent. The house's continued name changes may also point to this.

In March 1882, Captain F.W. Despard took a lease on the house and renamed it Donore. The new owners consisted of the captain, his invalid wife, four unmarried daughters, another married daughter who visited the house from time to time, and two sons, the eldest of whom was staying in a boarding school for most of the Despards tenancy. There were also three servants.

The family moved in at the end of April. Nothing happened until June, when 19-year-old Rosina Clara, the eldest unmarried daughter, retired to her room for the night. She heard someone outside her door and, thinking that it was her mother, opened it. No one was there. She fetched a candle and walked out into the passage, where she saw a tall woman standing at the top of the stairs. She was dressed in black and had a cap on her head. The lady held a handkerchief in front of her face. Her other hand was hidden by her sleeve and the fold of her dress. She appeared to be dressed as a widow. The figure then started to walk down the stairs. Rosina followed her, but the candle went out, so she returned to her room.

Rosina's married sister, Freda, also had a sighting in the summer of 1882. It was 6.30pm, and she was coming down the stairs from a first-floor bedroom when she saw a tall figure in black cross the hall and walk into the drawing room - she described her as being dressed like a Sister of Mercy. She asked the rest of the family, then seated in the dining room, about the woman but was told there was no such person. A servant was sent to the drawing room and found it deserted. They also confirmed that no one matching the figure's description had been allowed into the house.

Freda saw the figure on two more occasions: 'At another time I thought I saw her in the summer of 1884, looking in at the drawing room window from outside. This time the figure was not so distinct; the gas being lit in the room while it was semi-dark outside. Soon after, my sister, who had also seen her, saw her enter the room, but she was not then visible to me.

'I saw the figure once more in the spare room at night, having been awakened, as I constantly was, by footsteps in the room. I often heard footsteps at night up and downstairs, like a person wearing flat list or cloth slippers, and I have heard the swish of woollen drapery and, on several occasions, the sound of heavy bodies on the landings and against the doors, and overhead, the handles of doors turned, the sound of something heavy being dragged overhead, on the top storey. My husband and nurse have heard the same. I myself was much terrified at the sounds.'

In the autumn of 1883, a housemaid saw the same figure one night at approximately ten o'clock. She assumed someone had broken in and made an unsuccessful search of the house in an attempt to find her.

On December 18 of the same year, the woman in black was also seen by Wilfred, Rosina's six-year-old brother, and his friend. The time was approximately 3.15pm and they were playing on the terrace at the back of the house when they saw a woman crying through the window of the drawing room. She was holding a handkerchief to her face and was sitting at a writing table by the window. They went in but found the room empty. They asked the parlour maid about the woman, but she said that no one had entered the house.

Wilfred went on to see the ghost several more times. 'Once, when coming out of the drawing room, about half past eight (just after the gas had been lit throughout the house), I saw the figure going down the passage towards the side door, thus having her back to me. It finally disappeared in the direction of the kitchen stairs.

'The other time, on coming out of a room at the end of a passage on the first landing, I saw it going along the passage towards the staircase, but it turned back and finally disappeared through the door of another bedroom. This was about six o'clock in the evening; the gas not yet being lit, and so the light was somewhat dim.

'Another time I was in the morning room and had a momentary glimpse of the figure, but not long enough to be absolutely certain of having seen it. This was in the evening, the gas having been lit both in the room and in the passage outside.'

Wilfred also occasionally heard a sound like someone walking in soft slippers, but when he looked out, he saw no one. Sometimes the noises stopped, but at other times they would continue.

Rosina saw the same figure about a dozen times over the next two years. She noted that the top half of the figure appeared more distinct than the lower half. It would be seen going downstairs and entering the drawing room, where it would stand by the bow windows. Sometimes it would walk along the passage towards the garden at the front of the house, where it vanished. At first, Rosina had a feeling of awe at facing something unknown plus the desire to learn more about it. Later, she became conscious of a feeling of loss, almost as if she had lost power to the apparition. At first, she did not tell the rest of the family about her experiences and only confided the matter in letters to a friend, Catherine M. Campbell, who lived in the north of England.

Catherine even claimed to have had a vision, in which she found herself in the house watching the figure and Rosina walking down the stairs. She had not been told how the apparition was dressed prior to her vision, but her description – black dress, dark headgear, widow's cuffs, and a handkerchief – matched exactly the figure seen by Rosina. It emerged that Rosina had seen the woman in black on the same night as her friend's vision. Miss Campbell also visited the house in person and heard the footsteps. She confirmed that these were nothing like those of the family. The servants were excluded by the fact that they were changed during this time, yet the footsteps continued and were unaltered in character.

The sightings continued, with Rosina now trying to communicate with the figure: 'The first time I spoke to her was on the 29th of January 1884. I opened the drawing room door softly and went in, standing just by it. She came in past me and walked to the sofa, and stood still there, so I went up to her and asked her if I could help her. She moved, and I thought she was going to speak, but she only gave a slight gasp and moved towards the door. Just by the door, I spoke to her again, but she seemed as if she were quite unable to speak. She walked into the hall, then, by the side door, she seemed to disappear as before.

'I also attempted to touch her, but she always eluded me. It was not that there was nothing there to touch, but that she always seemed to be beyond me, and if followed into a corner, simply disappeared.

'During these two years, the only noises I heard were those of slight pushes against my bedroom door, accompanied by footsteps, and if I looked out on hearing these sounds, I invariably saw the figure. Her footstep is very light, you can hardly hear it, except on the linoleum, and then only like a person walking softly with thin boots on.'

On July 21, 1884, Rosina wrote, 'I went into the drawing room, where my father and sisters were sitting, about nine in the evening, and sat down on a couch close to the bow window. A few minutes after, as I sat reading, I saw the figure come in at the open door, cross the room, and take up a position close behind the couch where I was. I was astonished that no one else in the room saw her, as she was so very distinct to me. My youngest brother, who had before seen her, was not in the room. She stood behind the couch for about half an hour, and then, as usual, walked to the door. I went after her on the excuse of getting a book and saw her pass along the hall until she came to the garden door, where she disappeared. I spoke to her as she passed the foot of the stairs, but she did not answer, although as before, she stopped and seemed as though about to speak.'

On July 31, 1884, Edith, one of Rosina's sisters, told her that she had passed a woman on the stairs. Rosina suggested it was a servant, but inquiries proved none were in that area of the house at that time. Edith was to see and hear the apparition again: 'The next time

I saw the figure was one evening at about eight o'clock, in July 1885, a fine evening and quite light. I was sitting alone in the drawing room singing when suddenly I felt a cold, icy shiver, and I saw the figure bend over me, as if to turn over the pages of my song. I called my sister, who was in another room. She came at once and said she could see it still in the room, though I then could not.

'After coming up to bed one night in July 1886, my mother, myself, and one of the maids heard noises downstairs in the hall. On going down to investigate the cause, we saw nothing, and the noises ceased. After again returning to the top landing, the "noises" began again. It sounded as if people were throwing heavy articles, such as boots, across the passage and down the stairs. Door handles seemed to rattle too, the night being still and no one about. Two maids and my two sisters, and myself listened on the top landing, with lighted candles in our hands when we distinctly heard the footsteps pass and repass us quite close, but saw nothing, most of us feeling what we term the "icy shiver".

'I had just gone upstairs, on February 4th, 1887, to fetch some prescriptions for my father when I saw the same figure preceding me down the stairs. It went into the drawing room, which was then not being used. My father and I lighted a candle and stayed in the room for some little time, but saw nothing.'

Edith's description of the figure also matched the one seen by Rosina. She also noted that the woman's hands were long and very well-shaped.

The figure appeared again to Rosina on August 1, 1884: 'I heard the footsteps outside on the landing about 2am. I got up at once and went outside. She was then at the end of the landing at the top of the stairs, with her side view towards me. She stood there some minutes, then went downstairs, stopping again when she reached the hall below. I opened the drawing room door, and she went in, walked across the room to the couch in the bow window, stayed there a little, then came out of the room, went along the passage, and disappeared by the garden door. I spoke to her again, but she did not answer.'

Footsteps were heard the following night by three of Rosina's sisters and the cook. They were heard passing the bedrooms several times. The cook also said that she had heard the footsteps and had once seen a figure on the stairs after going down to get some hot water. The figure was described as tall and dressed in widow's clothes. Her face was hidden by a handkerchief held in her right hand. One morning, the cook also saw the figure through the kitchen window. She was standing on the garden terrace.

Rosina finally told her father about the ghost on August 5, 1884. He was described as being 'much astonished' as he had never seen or heard anything himself. The mother had also not seen anything, but this was attributed to her being infirm and hard of hearing.

Captain Despard asked the landlord if he had experienced anything strange in the house. But he denied having seen anything out of the ordinary during his three months living there.

On August 6, a neighbour, Annesley, a retired general, sent his son over to the house to ask about the lady he had seen in the orchard at the front of the building. She was described by him as 'a tall lady in black with a bonnet with a long veil, crying, with a handkerchief held up to her face.' He had assumed it was Rosina's married sister, Freda, who had recently lost a baby. Rosina confirmed that her sister had not been in the garden at the time.

Annesley visited the Despard's home that night in the hope of seeing the figure. The whole family took various positions in the house but did not see anything. However, that night, Rosina's sister and brother-in-law did hear footsteps on the stairs at 2am.

The apparition appeared again on August 11. It was dusk, and Rosina was in the drawing room with her married sister, two brothers, and a friend. Rosina and her sister saw the figure on the balcony outside the window. She stood there for several minutes and appeared to be looking into the room. She then walked to the end of the balcony and then back again. She then vanished. Soon after this, she appeared in the drawing room, but this time, only Rosina could see her. That evening, Edith saw the figure on the stairs as she left a room on the upper landing.

The sightings continued and were recorded by Rosina in her letters and in statements to Frederic Myers: 'The following evening, August 12th, while coming up the garden, I walked towards the orchard, when I saw the figure cross the orchard, go along the carriage drive in front of the house, and in at the open side door, across the hall, and into the drawing room, I following. She crossed the drawing room and took up her usual position behind the couch in the bow window. My father came in soon after, and I told him she was there. He could not see the figure but went up to where I showed him she was. She then went swiftly round behind him, across the room, out of the door, and along the hall, disappearing as usual near the garden door, we both following her. We looked out into the garden, having first to unlock the garden door, which my father had locked as he came through, but saw nothing of her.

'On August 12th, about 8pm, and still quite light, my sister E. was singing in the back drawing room. I heard her stop abruptly, come out into the hall, and call me. She said she had seen the figure in the drawing room, close behind her as she sat at the piano. I went back into the room with her and saw the figure in the bow window in her usual place. I spoke to her several times but had no answer. She stood there for about ten minutes or a quarter of an hour, then went across the room to the door and along the passage, disappearing in the same place by the garden door.

'My sister M. then came in from the garden, saying she had seen her coming up the kitchen steps outside. We all three then went out into the garden, when Mrs. K. called out from a window on the first storey that she had just seen her pass across the lawn in front and along the carriage drive towards the orchard. This evening, then, altogether four people saw her. My father was then away, and my youngest brother was out.

'On the morning of August 14th, the parlour maid saw her in the dining room, about 8.30am, having gone into the room to open the shutters. The room is very sunny, and even with all the shutters closed it is quite light, the shutters not fitting well, and letting sunlight through the cracks. She had opened one shutter when, on turning round, she saw the figure cross the room. We were all on the lookout for her that evening but saw nothing; in fact, whenever we had made arrangements to watch and were especially expecting her, we never saw anything.

'On August 16th, I saw the figure on the drawing room balcony, about 8.30pm. She did not afterwards come into the room, as on the former occasion. On looking out at the side door, nothing could be seen.

'The gardener said that he had seen the figure on the balcony that morning early, about six o'clock.

'On August 19th, three days after, we all went to the seaside, and were away a month, leaving three servants in the house.

'When we came back, they said that they had heard footsteps and noises frequently, but as the stair carpets were up part of the time and the house was empty, many of these noises were doubtless due to natural causes, though by them attributed to the figure.

'The cook also spoke of seeing the figure in the garden, standing by a stone vase on the lawn behind the house.'

The ghost continued to be seen throughout the rest of 1884 and the following year. The footsteps also continued to be heard; the most active months were July, August, and September.

Door handles were turned, and there were bumps against bedroom doors, which terrified one new servant, who thought burglars were breaking in. One servant, Mrs. Brown, saw the figure several times. In a statement made to Frederic Myers, she said, 'Some months after the thing became known. I was alone in the house one evening with Lizzie, a new cook (I do not know her address now), and we were standing at the door of the servants' hall, on the basement floor. The passage was lit with gas. Lizzie had heard nothing of the ghost, I am sure. Suddenly we both saw a dark, shadowy figure, dressed in black and making no noise, glide past us along the passage and disappear round a corner. Neither of us spoke as it passed, but directly after we looked at each other and each saw that the other had seen it, and we mentioned it to each other. We had seen just the same thing. I have myself never seen any white about the figure, but I know that others have seen her hold a handkerchief up to her face. The figure has never looked to me quite solid, but it has always vanished too quickly for me to look closely at it.

'The next time that I saw it was in the drawing room, when I went in to light the gas at dusk on a summer's evening. I saw a dark figure walk round the ottoman and disappear. I was not much frightened. The next time I saw no figure, but I was more frightened than any other time. I was going off the next day on a holiday, and I sat up late in my room with some sewing. My room was between Miss Morton's and the schoolroom, on the top floor, where the sounds were apt to be worst. I heard a loud noise, and looking up, I saw the handle of my door twisted round, as if someone were trying to come in. The door was locked, and this was not a mere slip of the handle. The handle was quite firm and never slipped off itself. I knew that no one was up or about, and I was motionless with fear. I could scarcely go to bed.

'Next morning, when I looked at myself in the glass, I saw that one side of my face was twisted by a slight stroke. I had been perfectly well the night before, and I could not believe that such a thing had happened. I thought it must be my fancy. But when I went downstairs, the other servants saw it. I went for my holiday, Saturday to Wednesday, and when I got back, I went at once to Dr. F., and he applied blisters to my face, and it gradually got straight again. He said that the twisted face might have been caused by a draught as well as by a fright – but I had been in no draught. I have no doubt that it was the fright, and for some time afterwards, my hand was very shaky and my nerves upset. But I went on with my work as usual, as I knew the thing could not really hurt me.

'I saw it twice more, both times in the drawing room. Once, it was as I was lighting the gas, as I had seen it before. The other time was when I entered the room in the morning and had taken down one shutter. I then saw it close by me, and was frightened, and called another servant to come to me. I stayed on in the place and was married from thence. One housemaid, while I was there, saw the figure, she said, on the road just outside the gates. She said that she saw her face.

'We often heard someone running down the steps from the approach to the back door and went to open the back door, and found no one there.

'I often heard noises on the attic landing, near my room – scuffling and knocking. Sometimes I would hear Miss Rose open her door and go downstairs. I know now that she was following the ghost. But I heard her before I knew about the ghost at all.'

The sound of someone walking up and down was heard on the second-floor landing and another set of footsteps was heard sometimes three or four nights a week. These sounds would last for the greater part of the night. These were centred on the bedroom once occupied by Henry and Imogen Swinhoe. They appeared to join the first set but were heavy and irregular. Other bumps and thuds were heard during summer in the vicinity of the room and on the upper landing. Things got so bad that several servants left and others would refuse to leave their bedrooms after dark.

In 1885, Frederic Myers, the investigator from the Society for Psychical Research (SPR), suggested that Rosina attempt to take a photograph of the apparition. However, the candlelight and the long exposure required for such a dark figure made the attempts impracticable. Rosina also continued to try to speak to the ghost and even asked her to make a sign if she could not speak, all without result. She tried to touch the figure, but it always vanished when cornered.

In the summer of 1886, Mrs. Twining, the family's charwoman, saw the figure while waiting in the hall one evening. She assumed it was a female visitor: 'I saw a lady pass by, rather tall, in black silk, with white collar and cuffs, a handkerchief in her hand, and a widow's fall. I had heard about the ghost, but it never struck me that this figure could be a ghost – it looked so like an ordinary person. I thought that someone had come to call and missed her way to the door. The family were at tea, and I was merely waiting, so out of curiosity, I followed the lady round the house. Just outside the morning room window, she suddenly disappeared. I was quite near her; it was quite impossible that a real person could have got away.

'I went into the house and began telling the housemaid that I had seen the ghost. She stopped me – pointing to the parlour maid, a new one whom they were anxious to keep in ignorance of the ghost – as the maids often left on account of it. The parlour maid had seen from one of the windows the same figure, though she had not known that it was the ghost. I believe that she left at the month's end.'

Rosina continued to make a written account of the haunting:, 'On one night in July 1886 (my father and I being away from home), my mother and her maid heard a loud noise in an unoccupied room over their heads. They went up, but seeing nothing and the noise ceasing, they went back to my mother's room on the first storey. They then heard loud noises from the morning room on the ground floor. They then went halfway downstairs, when they saw a bright light in the hall beneath. Being alarmed, they went up to my sister E., who then came down, and they all three examined the doors, windows, &c., and found them all fastened as usual. My mother and her maid then went to bed.

'My sister E. went up to her room on the second storey, but as she passed the room where my two sisters L. and M. were sleeping, they opened their door to say that they had heard noises and also seen what they described as the flame of a candle, without candle or hand visible, cross the room diagonally from corner to door. Two of the maids opened the doors of their two bedrooms and said that they had also heard noises; they all five stood at their doors with their lighted candles for some little time. They all heard steps walking up and down the landing between them; as they passed, they felt a sensation which they described as "a cold wind", though their candles were not blown about. They saw nothing. The steps then descended the stairs, re-ascended, again descended, and did not return.'

Rosina decided to gather evidence of any earlier psychic activity connected with the house.

She found out that a gardener who worked in a house opposite had seen a figure in their garden, a figure that 'he knew not to be a real person.' Rosina also met a lady at a friend's house who had lived in Cheltenham seven or eight years earlier. She had been told on several occasions that the house and garden were haunted by the second Mrs. Swinhoe. An officer who knew her uncle also remembered stories about the house being haunted and had often looked up at the windows when passing in the hope of seeing something.

It was at this time that the family got to hear about Mr. Swinhoe employing a carpenter to make a hiding place for his first wife's jewels under the floorboards in the morning room. Mr. Despard had the boards taken up but found the hiding place empty. He also thought that something may be hidden at the spot near the garden door where the ghost often appeared. However, a search found nothing.

Captain Despard decided to go to Bristol to look at the register of the second Mrs. Swinhoe's death. She had died from dipsomania and intervening sub-gastritis. He then spoke to her doctor and asked if Mrs. Swinhoe had suffered from any facial disfigurement, as this would explain why the figure constantly held a handkerchief to her face. The doctor said that her face was normal. However, he did confirm that Mrs. Swinhoe's face had become fuller and more rounded in the time that he had known her.

During the next two years, from 1887 to 1889, sightings of the apparition became less frequent. The louder noises also decreased, but the footsteps continued to be heard. From 1889 to 1892, the figure was not seen at all, and even the footsteps ceased. It should also be noted that the figure started to become less substantial as the years went on. In 1886 it had appeared solid but in later years became less so. It later emerged from Rosina's niece, Joyce Rynd, that her grandfather had the house exorcised by Canon Gardner of All Saints Church in the hope that it would quieten the ghost.

In 1948, a book on the haunting, *The Cheltenham Ghost*, was published by Psychic Press. The author, B. Abdy Collins, wrote of a solicitor, George Gooding, who had also seen the ghost several times during the Despards' tenancy. He referred to it as 'harmless' and spoke of it as 'a tall female figure dressed in black and with a handkerchief to her face as if crying.' The ghost appeared solid, and he recalled having once seen it in the garden in bright sunlight. He also saw it in the drawing room, 'when we made a ring round her by joining hands, from which she appeared merely to walk out between two people and then disappeared.' He also confirmed that the household dogs were very afraid of the figure. He believed that his godmother knew the identity of the ghost, having known the second Mrs. Swinhoe, but would never speak of her.

The Despards finally left the house in 1893, and Myers published his report in the journal of the SPR. Rosina went on to study at the London School of Medicine and qualified in 1895, a notable achievement for a woman in late-Victorian Britain. She retained an interest in psychical research and became a member of the SPR herself, carrying out experiments in thought transference with her friend Miss Campbell. The results of these were published in the SPR's journal. She died in 1930 and was buried in St James churchyard, Yarmouth, on the Isle of Wight.

As noted at the start of this chapter, Peter Underwood was not convinced that the house was haunted. He suggested that, as Mrs. Despard was an invalid, her husband had a mistress living in the house. He believed that the woman grew tired of being hidden away and sought exercise in the house and garden when the household was asleep or away. The figure's appearance in daylight was due to the woman taking advantage of the family being together in the dining room for a meal. Underwood also thought that the woman covered her face with the handkerchief to hide her identity. He also felt that too much reliance was placed on Rosina's record of the hauntings, as she was the sole witness to many of the strange things in the house.

Underwood also speculated that Rosina had suspicions as to the real-life nature of the 'ghost' and her father's relationship with it.

I have great admiration for Peter Underwood's vast body of work as a paranormal investigator, but on this occasion, I feel that he was wrong.

A ghost that is only seen by one person in a household full of people would, of course, prove unsatisfactory to the investigator, as questions would naturally be raised as to the truthfulness of the witness. But in this case, the figure was seen by at least seven members of the household. And why would Rosina happily write about the ghost to her friend if she suspected that it was really her father's lover? And why would Captain Despard openly talk about it to a friend and Frederic Myers if he was having an affair and wished it to remain secret? His only concern was the landlord and how talk of a ghost would affect the house's value, which was understandable as the property was only leased to him. And why would a woman staying secretly in the house then go out of her way to draw attention to herself by banging on doors, trying handles, and standing for minutes at a time in full view of the household? And what of the cold breeze felt by some members of the family when the ghost appeared?

Mrs. Sidgwick, who first mentioned the haunting in the SPR's journal in 1885, did consider the possibility that the ghost was a living person. However, she dismissed this theory, pointing out that it had 'once been seen by two together and on another occasion by one only, although others were present. This, and it apparently disappearing through a closed door, preclude the idea of it being any real person.' She also noted that the figure had been observed in different parts of the house at the same time, which would again rule out the notion that it was a living, breathing human being.

And let us also not forget that the house also had a reputation for being haunted before the Despards moved in. The apparition also appeared to be most active during July and August – the months in which Mr. Swinhoe and his first wife died. The description of the figure also resembled the second Mrs. Swinhoe. As Rosina Despard later told Frederic Myers, 'Although none of us had ever seen the second Mrs. S., several people who had known her identified her from our description. On being shown a photo album containing

Frederic Myers, a member of the SPR, investigated the Cheltenham haunting.

a number of portraits, I picked out one of her sister as being most like that of the figure, and was afterwards told that the sisters were much alike.'

Rosina also told Myers that Imogen Swinhoe's stepdaughter and others had told the family that her stepmother frequently used the front drawing room, the place where the figure continually appeared, and that her favourite seat was on a couch placed in a similar position to the one used by the Despards.

The figure was also seen to vanish when approached and, as already mentioned, appeared less solid as the years went on. It would also appear in a room when all the doors were closed. It should also be noted that attempts to detect fraud were made. Rosina tied a fine string across the stairs using marine glue. They were placed at different heights from the ground, ranging from 6in to 3ft. The string could not be felt by anyone walking on the stairs and could not be seen by candlelight from below. The slightest touch would have knocked the string down, and yet the figure was seen to pass through the string twice, leaving it undisturbed.

The dogs in the house also appeared to sense a presence. A large dog, a retriever, was kept in the kitchen and was once seen to emerge from the orchard terrified for no apparent reason. Another dog, a Skye terrier, was allowed to roam the house and often slept on Rosina's bed. Twice the dog was seen running up to an empty mat at the foot of the stairs in the hall, wagging its tail and jumping up as if waiting to be stroked. It would then retreat, shaking in fear, its tail between its legs. The family cat, however, never showed any signs of having seen the ghost.

Other writers have suggested that an underground stream was responsible for many of the noises heard in the house, the figure simply being water vapour. The stream causing some of the sounds is a distinct possibility, and even Rosina went on record as saying that certain noises could have been due to natural causes. However, the suggestion that the apparition was simply vapour caused by damp ignores the fact that witnesses clearly saw a clothed human figure.

Finally, the claim that the figure was really the secret lover of Captain Despard falls apart when we learn that the apparition continued to be seen for decades after Captain Despard and his family vacated the property. We will look at these sightings in the next chapter.

Chapter Seventeen

THE WOMAN IN BLACK: AFTER THE DESPARDS

The Despard family left their haunted home in 1893. The property remained empty for several years, but in 1898 it became a preparatory school for boys, its name being changed to Inholmes. Adby Collins, in his book *The Cheltenham Ghost*, was told by one correspondent that during this time the building was still haunted by the ghost. She appeared on the stairs, in the corridors, and even in the boys' sleeping area. She was also seen in broad daylight walking down the short drive. Maids left the school in terror, and one boy was so scared by her that he almost died. These continued sightings apparently played a part in the school closing some nine years later.

In 1910, the house became a nuns' residence, and a chapel was added to the building. In 1912, it was renamed St. Anne's Nursery College and became a centre for training nannies until 1935, when it was taken over by the Diocese of Gloucester as a conference centre and a retreat. This closed in 1970, and in 1973, the building was purchased by the Cheltenham Housing Association and converted into flats. The adjoining grounds were sold, and several bungalows were built there.

In 1958, Percy Wilson, a spiritualist, interviewed a Mrs. Maisley who lived in the town. She claimed to have seen a ghost many times in the garden of St. Anne's in the early 1920s. Mrs. Wilson's father had also seen the ghost, as had her uncle George, who had later moved to the USA. George told the couple that he had often seen the apparition: 'We used to go and see the ghost dancing across the lawn on many occasions when I was a boy. It used to be quite a common experience with the boys of the town.' He described the figure as 'just a lady, who walked and sort of danced, if not floated, across the lawn'.

Wilf Cox, who later became an author, visited the house during the occupation of the Diocesan Council and spoke to the warden. He claimed no knowledge of the haunting and said that he had witnessed nothing out of the ordinary during his time there. Mr. Cox and his wife explored the house but saw nothing. However, several cold spots were

The Cheltenham apparition (from The Cheltenham Ghost by B. Abdy Collins).

noted in various parts of the building. Night vigils were held outside, but nothing out of the ordinary was observed.

In the autumn of 1969, a clergyman was staying in the house during a residential weekend. He was unaware that the building was said to be haunted. After evensong, his colleagues decided to go to a local hotel for a drink, but he decided to stay in the house and have an early night as he had a cold coming on. At approximately 10.45pm, he was awoken by a strange sound and the sensation of fingers scratching the eiderdown across the back of his neck. He assumed it was someone playing a practical joke and sat up. The room was empty and extremely cold. He then saw, to his amazement, the bedclothes being pulled to the floor. He started to say a prayer, and, as he did so, a grey shape began to appear by the door. It drifted slowly towards him, passed over his head, and went through the wall. He put on the light and searched the house. He was alone. He assumed that his experience had been brought on by his cold and said nothing to the other clergymen when they returned.

In 1970, the clergyman was at Wells Theological College. One evening, a colleague who was also a member of the Society for Psychical Research started to talk about the ghost that haunted St. Anne's. He was amazed by this and decided to tell of his own experience, discovering that another clergyman, now dead, had an almost identical sighting to his. It emerged that he had slept in the old main bedroom, and the wall - the one the ghost had gone through - originally had a connecting door to the old dressing room. Alterations in that part of the house had caused the door to be blocked.

Andrew Mackenzie, an author and member of the SPR, wrote of the Cheltenham haunting several times. He discovered that a nearby house had been haunted by a figure that closely resembled the woman in black. He interviewed the witnesses and obtained three signed statements from the men, detailing what they had seen.

In October 1958, John Thorne, who was a sales manager at a brewery, was living in an apartment in Cotswold Lodge (now demolished and replaced by flats), which stood near St. Anne's on the opposite side of the road. He awoke one night at approximately 2.30am and saw a woman standing between the bed and the window. She appeared to be watching him. He hid under the bedclothes but looked out again to see the woman still standing there. The woman was of average height and was wearing a long, Victorian-looking dress. He hid under the bedclothes again and tugged at his wife's nightdress. She turned on the light but saw no one. She said that he must have been dreaming, but he was not convinced by her explanation. They decided to keep the matter to themselves and told no one.

Mr. Thorne also noticed that twice during their tenancy, the doorbell rang when no one was there. An inspection of the device ruled out an electrical fault. However, he did not rule out a physical reason for its ringing. He also confirmed that he had never heard of the ghost said to haunt St. Anne's.

John's brother William, William's wife Paulette, their 15-year-old son, and their four-year-old daughter stayed overnight at the flat in late November 1961. Paulette and the daughter shared a bedroom, and William and his son shared a couch in the drawing room. Although four heaters had been burning, both noticed that the drawing room had become very cold.

The family had gone to bed just before midnight. The moon was out, and the curtains were left open. Ten minutes later, as William started to fall asleep, he heard heavy, muffled footsteps in the corridor. He thought it was Paulette, and called out, 'Is that you, Paulette?' There was no response.

He then looked at the open door and saw a woman in a long black dress that looked Victorian. She was holding a handkerchief to her face. She was about 5ft 2in tall and her head was faintly outlined by light. Her hair seemed to be tied in a bun that appeared light-coloured or golden. The figure was solid, but the upper part was more defined than the lower. The woman was looking into the room, but not directly at him.

He closed and opened his eyes several times, but the figure was still standing there, some six or seven feet from him. He was not scared but did feel as if he was 'in a state of trance'.

John, his son, heard his father say, 'Is that you, Paulette?' He lifted himself up on his right elbow and looked over his shoulder to see the woman standing there. She was completely outlined in phosphorescence, and he noted that her long dress covered her feet. He did not notice the handkerchief but thought that she had her hair tied in a bun. He did not feel scared and asked his father if he could see her too. William confirmed that he could and asked him to close the door. The figure vanished as he got up. He looked up and down the corridor but could see no one.

Paulette and her daughter, sleeping in the bedroom, saw nothing. However, the mother had spent a restless night, and, despite having hot water bottles in the bed, she had felt very cold.

William decided not to tell Paulette about the figure, as she often was alone in the flat, and he only told his brother about seeing the ghost after they had returned to their own home.

In 1970, Mrs. Jackson, who was taking a lunchtime driving lesson, saw a tall figure dressed in a long black dress appear and step off the kerb as she was driving past St. Anne's. Mrs. Jackson did an emergency stop, which surprised the instructor as he had not seen the figure himself.

A postman had a similar experience when cycling past the house. A lady suddenly appeared on the pavement, and he had to swerve to avoid hitting her. The woman then vanished.

One of the first couples to move into a flat in the Despards former home experienced several strange things during their six years there. One Boxing Day, the husband arrived home at 10pm and saw a female figure gliding down the stairs. She was described as being dressed in grey with fair hair hanging down her back and appearing to be 35 to 40 years old.

The couple's sitting room occupied the old nursery. An 8ft shelf once fell from the wall despite being fixed to it with six brackets. Pictures would also fly off the wall, leaving the hooks in place with the picture cords still draped over them.

Objects, especially clothing, would vanish only to reappear in other parts of the flat, and the lights in a fish tank would switch on and off by themselves. A large vine would also move as if someone had brushed past it. The couple also learned that workmen renovating the house had seen a female figure walking down the front steps.

Another tenant who occupied a flat on the lower floor once saw two elderly ladies vanish on the stairs.

In 1979, a dog was found motionless but still alive in one of the bungalows built in the former garden of the house. A vet was called, and it was found that the animal had suffered a minor heart attack. The vet said that it had been caused by shock. It will be remembered that during the tenancy of the Despards, the dogs were seen to exhibit fear after apparently encountering the ghost.

In July 1985, an Oxford University music graduate and a friend were walking along Pittville Circus Road. The time was approximately 10pm. They suddenly saw a tall woman dressed in black crinoline moving along the footpath of St Anne's Close towards the junction with the main road. They were both intrigued by the woman's old-fashioned clothing and walked back but found that she had vanished.

Strange things are still said to occur in the house. It seems that the mysterious Woman in Black is not ready to move on.

Chapter Eighteen

THE HAUNTING OF BERRY POMEROY CASTLE

Berry Pomeroy Castle in Devon is a ruined Tudor mansion that lies within the walls of an earlier castle. The de la Pomeroy family originally held the land following the Norman conquest, but in 1547 Edward Seymour, the first Duke of Somerset and Lord Protector to the young King Edward VI, bought the castle from them. He did not enjoy his new home for long, as he was accused of treason and beheaded in 1552, his lands being taken by the Crown. In 1558, Lord Edward Seymour, his son by his first marriage gained title to the castle and built a new house within the old defensive walls. The Seymour family continued to live at Berry Pomeroy, but by the 18th century, the house was in a poor state of repair, and Edward, the fourth Baronet, decided to erect a new home at Maiden Bradley in Wiltshire. His old home was stripped of building materials, and it became a ruin. The castle is still owned by the Duke of Somerset but is now administered by English Heritage.

Drawn by W. Westall A.R.A.

Engraved by E. Finden

BERRY POMEROY CASTLE, DEVONSHIRE.

Berry Pomeroy is regarded as one of the most haunted castles in Britain. Deryck Seymour, in his book *The Ghosts of Berry Pomeroy Castle*, estimates that over 80 people in the last few decades have witnessed unexplained phenomena there.

People visiting the castle often start to feel depressed or fearful upon reaching the gatehouse. Some note a sense of evil and even feel that the ruins intend to do them harm. Jack Hazzard, a foreman for the Ministry of the Environment, would often notice visitors suddenly leave in fear. Others would start to feel ill, drained of all their energy, and find that they had trouble walking. One child even ran back to her mother to say, 'Something horrid had touched my hair!' Cameras, lights, and filming equipment frequently fail in the castle grounds despite having worked perfectly outside. Batteries are often found completely drained of power, and sometimes even car engines have been affected.

Mrs. Hartshorn and her friends, Mr. and Mrs. Fore, visited the castle one night and had a terrifying experience. They were on the path leading to the gatehouse when they saw a small white cloud hanging over the building. A faint, bluish light was coming from one of the windows, and the air was filled with hostility - a force that seemed to be willing them to leave. Another light appeared below the other, and the three friends rushed back to their car. They looked again before leaving and again saw the light. The cloud had moved to the right and then back again as if, according to Mr. Fore, it was following them.

Miss White of Torquay told the author, Judy Chard, of some friends who had seen some ruined cottages and derelict barns near the castle. There was a sense of evil in the air, and one member of the group returned to the car extremely upset. They returned a few days later and were amazed to see the very same cottages, complete with well-tended gardens. Had they witnessed a time slip on their first visit, a glimpse into the past or even the future when the cottages were abandoned to ruin?

In the summer of 1982, Mr. and Mrs. Hills and their ten-year-old son took separate helicopter flights over the castle. All saw the castle restored to its former glory with turrets, pinnacles, and pitched roofs. Smoke was also seen to rise from the chimneys. They later visited the castle and were surprised to find it a ruin.

Visitors to Berry Pomeroy often report hearing the slamming of heavy wooden doors in places where no such door has existed for centuries.

Another time slip was experienced by Miss E. Beveridge, who was visiting Castle Mill one May afternoon with a South African friend. They drove into a lane, but after half a mile or so, an uncomfortable silence descended upon them. Both became conscious of a strange and disturbing atmosphere. Chickens were scratching in a field, but the breed, scraggy, long-legged birds, was unknown to them. The chicken houses were also made of turf, straw, and branches.

The pair were both struck by the total silence as they drove on. They turned a corner and found themselves in a small farmyard with a thatched and shabby mill house, several

Berry Pomeroy Castle, Banquet Hall

run-down sheds, and a stream. A few ducks were on the edge of the water, and a young girl of 11 or 12 was crouching on a low wall. She was dirty, with swarthy skin and rough black hair. She was wearing a sack with holes cut into it for the legs and arms, and a rope was tied around her waist. Her black eyes gazed at the pair with intense hatred. Both women became scared, and they turned the car around in the yard and drove back up the lane, the girl glaring at them as they did so. Both felt that they had experienced something from another time.

Despite her fear, Miss Beveridge decided to go back there two weeks later with her cousin Katie, although she did not mention her earlier visit to her relative. They walked into the lane and reached the spot where the atmosphere had suddenly changed before. Katie decided to wait, and so Miss Beveridge went on alone. This time everything was different. The air was filled with the sounds of farmyard animals, and she saw a man whistling as he crossed a field with his sheepdog. Modern-looking hen houses had replaced the ones from her previous visit, and none of the hens resembled the strange breed from before. The mill house roof had been rethatched, and there was now a second storey. A new wing and porch had also been added, and there were leaded windows where before there had been just holes.

Miss Beveridge returned to Katie, who looked relieved, as she had been worried that she would never see her relative again. She now admitted that she had been afraid to go on as she had sensed something strange about the place.

There is a legend of two Pomeroy sisters, Eleanor and Margaret, who lived in the castle and were in love with the same man. The elder, Eleanor, was extremely jealous of Margaret as she was the more beautiful. Eleanor locked Margaret up in the castle's bottom-most dungeon, where she died of starvation. Her ghost now walks the ramparts in long white robes and supposedly calls on those who witness her to follow her to their deaths in the dungeon.

The author, Chips Barber, recalled playing football in the castle as a boy in the 1960s. The ball was kicked over the castle ramparts and bounced down a flight of steps into St. Margaret's Tower. He went to fetch it and felt the presence of someone close to him. He turned to see someone in a long, flowing dress disappearing up the steps. The castle was closing, and he told the custodian that he had seen a lady in the tower, but it emerged that no one else had seen her leave. A search of the castle grounds found no one matching her description.

Peter Kirk was looking around the castle with his wife. It was dusk, and they were walking along the Rampart Walk towards St. Margaret's Tower. Mrs. Kirk decided to wait as she began to feel scared. Her husband went on and climbed the tower staircase. He then felt the urge to visit the dungeon when he was shocked to see the White Lady standing before him. He rushed back to his wife, and they left the ruins. He only told her what he had seen when they reached the castle's tea room. Neither of them had heard of the legend of the White Lady before their visit.

Another sighting of the White Lady occurred in April 1987, when Warren Hunt visited the castle one night on his own. He found himself in the dungeon, which suddenly became filled with a blinding light. Standing in front of him was the apparition of a woman dressed in white. It is not surprising to learn that he too fled the scene, leaving his car, which he had to retrieve the following day. He vowed never again to visit Berry Pomeroy.

Hillary Philips visited the castle with her four children. She decided to view the dungeon in the southern tower of the gatehouse with her son, Dominic. As they descended the steps, she became frightened and felt as if tight bands had been placed on her head. She grabbed her son, and they rushed out. The boy was also upset and described having the same sensation as his mother.

A similar experience to this was had by Mr. D.W. Roddy when he and his brother visited the castle as children. They were climbing St. Margaret's Tower when they both felt pressure on their temples and became scared. Several years later, Mr. Roddy returned to Berry Pomeroy with some friends. It was about 12.30am when they saw a small, dim blue light drifting across the top of the ramparts. He again felt the sensation of pressure on his temples and fled the castle, vowing never to return there.

On Midsummer's Eve in 1983, Craig Rowland went to Berry Pomeroy at midnight with some friends. They all heard the sound of tramping feet in the undergrowth behind them. Although the moon was shining brightly, they could see no one. Craig then saw the White Lady walking along the Rampart Walk, ran back to the car, and drove off, leaving his friends to run after him. They finally caught up with him and learned of his experience. It appeared that only Craig had seen the phantom.

Hamlyn Parsons told the author Theo Brown how Bruno, his cocker spaniel, would always go mad with fear whenever they approached St. Margaret's Tower. Even attempts to carry the animal in his arms while facing away from the tower would bring on the same reaction. Other dogs have also shown fear when approaching the tower. One couple on their honeymoon went to the castle in September with their dog. They were walking along Rampart Walk towards St Margaret's Tower when they suddenly entered a patch of freezing air, which made the hair on their heads stand up. They saw nothing but their dog, which became terrified and ran off howling.

A psychic medium visited the castle one night, parking up in front of the gatehouse. Her car was shaken by unseen forces, and she saw a figure in white walking along the Rampart Walk.

Another story concerns an 18th-century doctor, Walter Farquhar, who encountered a ghost known as the Blue Lady at Berry Pomeroy. He had been called to attend the wife of the steward of the castle. He was waiting in the parlour when the door opened, and a young lady dressed in blue, wringing her hands in distress, swept past him and, after a brief pause, walked up the oak staircase. As she reached the top step, the light from the window fell on her face. She was young and beautiful, but her face exhibited agony and remorse.

The next day, he told the steward about the woman. The man looked shocked and became convinced that his wife would die. The doctor tried to reassure him that his wife was getting better, but the steward refused to listen. He explained that the ghost was a Pomeroy daughter who had been made pregnant by her father. When the baby was born, she smothered it in an upstairs room. Since then, she has always appeared before the death of anyone living in the castle. She had been seen on the very day that his son had drowned, and her appearance before the doctor was sure to herald his wife's passing. He was sadly proved correct, for she died the very same day. It is also recorded that the ghost was seen before the death of the steward. Sometimes the cries of the Blue Lady's baby are also heard.

Heather Reilly, a nurse, visited the castle one autumn night in 1982 with three girlfriends. It was raining, and as they drove by the gatehouse, they saw that it was barred by a portcullis. They parked the car and walked towards the gate. They were surprised to see that the portcullis had vanished. In its place was a slatted gate. Due to the rain, they sheltered under the gatehouse, and at approximately 1am, Miss Reilly heard the sounds of a baby crying. The sounds seemed to be coming from a nearby wood. The crying continued on and off for some 15 minutes, then stopped. It emerged that none of her friends had heard the baby.

Elliott O'Donnell wrote of an army officer who attempted to rescue a young woman dressed in blue who was calling to him from the ramparts. He started to climb towards her but was nearly killed when some of the stonework gave way. He managed to cling to

a narrow ledge, where he was finally spotted and rescued from an almost certain death. He told his rescuers of the lady trapped on the battlements but was told not to worry as she was a ghost who took delight in trying to lure people, especially men, to their deaths.

Shelia Ellis, who used to be in charge of the castle's tea room, knew of a clergyman, his wife, and their 18-year-old daughter who had visited the castle grounds. As they were passing through the gatehouse, the daughter suddenly fainted. When she recovered, she spoke of having seen a young woman, wearing blue, who beckoned to her from the gateway. Her face had such an expression of evil that she passed out from shock.

The Blue Lady was seen again in 1980 by Jane Everitt, who was looking around the castle with her friends. It was 2pm, and the group was leaving by a steep path when Mrs. Everitt looked back and saw a female figure, dressed in blue or purple, watching them from the window of one of the top-storey rooms at the back of the castle. Her friends could not see the figure, and she realised it must be a ghost as there was no floor for the woman to stand on.

Mr. and Mrs. Hills saw a very different ghost in December 1908. It was 8.30pm and they were driving near the castle when they saw a man dressed as a cavalier cross the road in front of them. He was wearing a large hat with a feather, a doublet and hose, and had a bushy moustache that curled up at the ends. He was walking at a higher level than the modern road and smiled at them as he did so. Mrs. Hills then received a message telepathically from him that he was going to the hostelry. Two weeks later, Mrs. Hills was on the same road and saw the figure again. The time was 4.45pm. He was walking away from the castle and gazed at her as she passed him. This time, she received no telepathic message.

Robert Graves (Figgis-West).

Aya Broughton, an artist of some repute, was in the castle grounds with her husband one summer afternoon. She was in the courtyard painting, as her husband had gone for a walk. The place was deserted, and the silence seemed uncanny. Even the brightness of the light seemed unusual. Suddenly, a flock of nesting birds flew into the air, crying out in alarm. She then became aware of a large black hound who was pacing up and down before her. There was no sign of the owner, and, being psychic, she realised that this was no living creature. A sense of evil came from the thing, and, trying to remain calm, she began to recite a Buddhist prayer for use in the presence of evil spirits. As she did so, the animal faded away.

Two young knights, the sons of Henry Pomeroy, held the castle in 1549 during the so-called Prayer Book Rebellion, in which large parts of the population in the South West rose in protest at the religious changes enforced by the boy king, Edward VI. Rather than see the castle sacked by the besieging army, they hid the family gold and other valuables in the castle before blindfolding their horses and leaping over the cliff to their deaths in the valley below. The area became known as Pomeroy's Leap, and the sounds of horses galloping and screams can still be heard in the area from time to time. Professor Raymond Cattell wrote in his book, *Under Sail Through Red Devon,* of hearing the sound 'of hoofbeats during a visit to the castle'.

A young man named Nokes once dreamed on three successive nights that he would find the hidden treasure in one of the castle's ruined fireplaces. He told a local doctor, who advised him to look the next day. Nokes went to the castle the next morning and found one of the fireplaces had been broken into. He could see nothing inside but later discovered that the doctor had suddenly become very rich.

Mr. Upton from Paignton was riding his motorbike along the lane beneath Pomeroy's Leap when the machine suddenly went out of control, throwing him into a ditch. He could find no reason for the crash, as there was no fault with the bike and the road was not even wet. His wife, as a young girl, had visited the castle with her parents. Her mother had become lost in the cellars and started to become frightened as she could not find her way out. Suddenly, a woman in white appeared and pointed to the stairs and the exit. She told the curator of her odd experience, who gave her a strange look and said that no one else had entered the castle during their visit.

Robert Graves, the author of such classic novels as *I Claudius* and *Claudius the God,* wrote of seeing a photograph taken at Berry Pomeroy by a certain Mrs. Beer. It showed a tall woman in 14th-century clothing walking by the gate. She was leading a small ape on a chain. The lady gave the photograph to Graves, but he burned it because 'it was too horrible'.

A wishing tree stands in the castle grounds. You are supposed to whisper your wish to the beech tree and then walk backwards around it three times. As long as you do not tell anyone your wish, it will come true.

Chapter Nineteen

PENGERSICK CASTLE
BY JASON FIGGIS

Cornwall is a county situated in the picturesque South West of England. It is recognised as one of the Celtic nations and the homeland of the Cornish people. Cornwall is bordered to the north and west by the Celtic Sea, to the south by the English Channel, and to the east by the county of Devon, with the River Tamar forming the border between them. The county also forms the westernmost part of the South West Peninsula of the island of Great Britain and is a land steeped in legend and mystery.

It was home to Colin Wilson, one of Britain's greatest writers. Among his almost 200 published books and thousands of articles, he was also the author of the celebrated works *The Outsider* and *The Occult*, both of which have never been out of print.

It was on a trip to this beautiful county in 2002 with my father, Peter, and then partner, Ann Murray, that I called in to visit Colin at his home near Gorran Haven. It was a wonderful experience to sit with him while he read me the opening chapter of his memoir,

Dreaming to Some Purpose, which was published a year later. During our chat, we discussed the wealth of Cornwall's historic treasures and, in particular, its rich heritage of ghost stories. He made a strong argument for visiting as many of the haunted sites as possible during our visit, and as my small party took our leave, I was determined to find places of particular interest in the county.

One of these was Pengersick Castle.

Pengersick is a fortified manor house located between the villages of Germoe and Praa Sands. The tower house, which is situated in the parish of Breige, is a grade one-listed building of an impressively austere appearance, with parts dating from the early 1500s. It is also believed to be one of the most haunted buildings in the British Isles.

The writer Sabine Baring-Gould penned the following about Pengersick: 'Near Germoe, but nearer the sea, is a very fine remnant of a castle, Pengersick. It was erected in the time of Henry VIII by a man named Millaton, probably of Millaton in Bridestow, Devon. He had committed murder, and to escape justice, he fled his native county and hid in the dip of land facing the sea at Pengersick, where he constructed an amply protected tower. The basement is furnished with loops for firing upon anyone approaching, and above the door is a shoot for melted lead. The entire building is beautifully constructed. Here, Millaton remained in concealment until he died, never leaving his tower for more than a brief stroll. The land had not been purchased in his own name but in that of his son Job. Job was made governor of Saint Michael's Mount, and his son, William, was made sheriff of Cornwall in 1565 and married Honor Godolphin, daughter of Sir William Godolphin.'

The ghost of the poet John Milton is said to haunt the castle, and so with this history and potential supernatural experience to be had, we set off for a two-night stay in the beautiful bed and breakfast adjacent to the very impressively preserved Pengersick Castle.

Several incidents occurred.

The first experience had its first part innocently played out when my father, Peter, chose a very comfortable bedroom with a view of the castle itself. He sat in the window seat several times throughout the evening and night, admiring the castle walls and battlements from his vantage point by the window, but this is where the second chapter played out when the sun rose on a perfect morning the following day. My father's first instinct was to go to the window for a fresh view of the surrounding countryside, and he was more than startled to realise that the castle was no longer visible. He sat in the chair, as he had on the previous evening and night, and strained for a view, even adjusting the chair to attempt some kind of manipulation of the vista beyond.

There was little point, as the castle was nowhere to be seen.

When he went outside to investigate, needless to say, the castle was where it had always been, but when he looked up to the window of his bed and breakfast room, he could see quite clearly that a view of any part of the castle would have been utterly impossible.

Jason Figgis and his father chatting with the former owner of Pengersick Castle (Ann Murray).

We have never been able to explain this bizarre phenomenon.

The evening of our second night's stay saw a party of ghost hunters, led by a local writer and a monk medium, arrive at the castle for the purposes of a night vigil. The writer could see our enthusiasm, but as it was a private booking, he offered us a tour after the former party's departure in the early hours of the following morning. We readily agreed.

So it was that at 2am, we entered the stone spiral to ascend to the upper rooms where the majority of supernatural experiences had been recorded.

Peter, Ann, and I stood in the company of the author and monk medium in the main bedroom of Pengersick as the medium spoke softly and with great clarity to any spirits that may have been present. Almost immediately, the room became icy cold, and the medium inhaled deeply and smiled. We saw nothing, but a presence was most definitely felt by all. The medium gasped lightly as he described the sensation of a cold hand brushing off his own.

We stayed in the castle for about an hour, but as we descended the winding spiral to the ground, we were all overcome by a dreadful stench as we approached the final bend that led to the door.

We exited as quickly as we could and all stared up at the very imposing structure as the summer sun began to break the canopy of trees and shine golden upon its thick grey walls.

We drove away later that morning to continue our Cornwall adventure and discussed and shared our mutual experiences of the previous two days in a place that we felt was undeniably haunted but wonderful to behold.

FINALLY...

Alisdair Alpin MacGregor, the author of two wonderful books on the supernatural, wrote of a Devon mansion where a young woman was a guest. The year was 1936. She was alone one evening in a lower room when she saw a young man enter through a door to her left. He looked at her hard, and she returned his gaze. He then left through another door to her right. His appearance interested her, and she asked her hostess who he was. She described the man to her in detail, but no one there matched his description.

Two years later, she was in London when she met the very same man! She explained to him that they had met before in Devon. He denied this and said that he had never heard of the mansion. The two became friends and then lovers. They eventually married and were invited to the very mansion where she had first seen him. They arrived in the evening, and the lady decided to show her husband the room of her vision. He looked around in amazement and insisted that he had never seen the house before this visit. He then walked out of the second door and vanished. A search of the house was made, but he was nowhere to be found. The BBC even put out a description of him on the radio without success. He was never seen again.

Happy ghost hunting!

FURTHER READING

Chapter One
Strange But True (1994); Jenny Randles and Peter Hough

Chapter Two
Haunted Dover (2009); Lorraine Sencicle

Chapter Three
Ghosts and Legends of Wales (1987); J.A. Brooks
Ghosts of Suffolk (1998); Betty Puttick
Norfolk: A Ghosthunter's Guide (2007); Neil Story
Ghosts Caught on Film (2007); Dr. Melvyn Willin

Chapter Four
Paranormal Norfolk (2010); Frank Meeres
Gazetteer of British Ghosts (1971); Peter Underwood

Chapters Five and Six
Titanic: Psychic Forewarnings of a Tragedy (1988); George Behe
The Wreck of the Titanic Foretold? (1986); Martin Gardiner

Chapter Seven
Yorkshire Oddities, Incidents, and Strange Events (1874); S. Baring-Gould

Chapter Eight
The Ghost Book (1955); Alasdair Alpin MacGregor
Paranormal Suffolk (2009); Christopher Reeve

Chapter Nine

The Mask of Time (1978); Joan Forman

Adventures in Time (1997) Andrew MacKenzie

Chapter Ten

Strange But True? Casebook (1995); Jenny Randles

Chapter Eleven

Supernatural North (2009); Darren W. Ritson

Chapter Twelve

Ghosts of London (1975); Jack Hallam

Haunted London (1973); Peter Underwood

Chapter Thirteen

Ghosts Helpful and Harmful (1924); Elliott O'Donnell

Chapter Fourteen

Dangerous Ghosts (1954); Elliott O'Donnell

Haunted Churches (1939); Elliott O'Donnell

Chapter Fifteen

Lord Halifax's Ghost Book (1936); Charles Wood, 2nd Viscount Halifax

Haunted Houses (1907); Charles G. Harper

Hauntings (1977); Peter Underwood

Chapters Sixteen and Seventeen

The Cheltenham Ghost (1948) B. Adby Collins

Hauntings and Apparitions (1982) Andrew Mackenzie.

Cheltenham, Town of Shadows (1988) Bob Meredith

Record of a Haunted House, Proceedings of the Society for Psychical Research 8, pp. 311-32. (1892); R.C. Morton

Hauntings (1977); Peter Underwood

Chapter Eighteen

Devon Stories of the Supernatural (2003); Judy Chard

The Ghosts of Berry Pomeroy Castle (1990); Deryck Seymour

Chapter Nineteen

Mysterious Cornwall (2008); Rupert Matthews

More recommended reading

Haunted Britain (1973); Antony D. Hippisley Coxe

Ghosts of Today (1980); Andrew Green

The Midnight Hearse and More Ghosts (1965); Elliott O'Donnell

This Haunted Isle (1984); Peter Underwood

The Penguin Book of Ghosts (2008); Westward and Simpson

The Master Ghost Hunter (2016); Richard Whittington-Egan

Other books by John West

Roman Lincoln (1991)

Oliver Cromwell and the Battle of Gainsborough (1992)

Studies in Scarlet (1994)

Roman York (1995)

Roman Lincoln (second edition, 1998)

Britain's Haunted Heritage (2019)

Britain's Ghostly Heritage (2022)

The Battle of Gainsborough (2022)

ND - #0319 - 270225 - C0 - 234/156/11 - PB - 9781780916439 - Gloss Lamination